# THE BRITISH EMPIRE
### AND
# THE UNITED STATES

# THE BRITISH EMPIRE

### AND

# THE UNITED STATES

A REVIEW OF THEIR RELATIONS DURING THE CEN-
TURY OF PEACE FOLLOWING THE TREATY OF GHENT

BY

## WILLIAM ARCHIBALD DUNNING

LIEBER PROFESSOR OF HISTORY AND POLITICAL PHILOSOPHY
IN COLUMBIA UNIVERSITY
SOMETIME PRESIDENT OF THE AMERICAN HISTORICAL ASSOCIATION

WITH AN INTRODUCTION BY

THE RIGHT HONOURABLE VISCOUNT BRYCE, O.M.

AND A PREFACE BY

NICHOLAS MURRAY BUTLER

PRESIDENT OF COLUMBIA UNIVERSITY

NEW YORK

CHARLES SCRIBNER'S SONS

1914

KRAUS REPRINT CO.
New York
1969

L.C. Catalog Card Number 14-18567.


COPYRIGHT, 1914, BY
CHARLES SCRIBNER'S SONS

Published October, 1914

KRAUS REPRINT CO.
A U.S. Division of Kraus-Thomson Organization Limited

Printed in U.S.A.

## PREFACE

UNDER the happiest auspices and with the hearty co-operation of the leaders of opinion throughout the British Empire and in the United States, plans have been made for an adequate and dignified celebration of the impressive fact that for one hundred years the English-speaking peoples throughout the world have been at peace with one another. The impressiveness of this fact is heightened by the circumstances leading up to and attending the American Revolution and by those which relate to the War of 1812. With the exception of the short contest of 1898 with Spain, which contest had its origin in purely American conditions, the United States has been not only at peace, but usually in the friendliest possible relations with Germany, France, Russia, Italy, and the other nations of continental Europe. On the other hand, there have been many and frequent occasions when public opinion, either in Great Britain or in the United States, or in both, has been deeply stirred by some difference of view or by some incident of diplomatic controversy. There have been more tempting occasions for misunderstanding and armed conflict between the British Empire and the United States than between the United States and all other nations of the earth combined. The points of contact between the British Empire and the United States are many, and each point of contact is a point of possible friction. Their commercial interests are often in keen rivalry. In times past their territorial ambitions have been in sharp conflict with each other. Notwithstanding, a full hundred years has passed during which war between them has been avoided. This fact is of itself an eloquent testimony to the temper and self-restraint of the English-speaking peoples and a noble tribute to the statesmen who have in succession guided their policies and conducted their international business. The long invisible line which separates the United States and the Dominion of Canada has been left unguarded despite the fact that two energetic, rapidly expanding peoples have been pushing steadily westward on either side of it. This long, invisible, unguarded line is the most convincing testimony that the world has to offer to the ability of modern self-disciplined peoples to keep the peace. It affords an example which it is not unreasonable to hope may one day be universally followed.

As part of the celebration of one hundred years of peace between the British Empire and the United States, the committees in charge planned a historical review of the relations between the two countries since the signing of the Treaty of Ghent. This delicate and difficult task was committed to William Archibald Dunning, Lieber Professor of History and Political Philosophy in Columbia University, and at the time President of the American Historical Association. With what clearness, cogency, and impartiality Professor Dunning has fulfilled his task the pages that follow amply testify. It has been his purpose to

". . . Nothing extenuate,
Nor set down aught in malice. . . ."

He has made no attempt to minimize or to gloss over the differences that have arisen between the two peoples, the grounds or causes for those differences, or the errors of judgment that may have been committed in attempting to resolve them. The result is a survey of the past century which is full of encouragement for those who are longing for the day when justice and not force shall rule the destinies of the world. If disputes such as are here traced and recounted can be adjusted without war; if differences of temperament, of ambition, and of interest such as are here described can be settled without armed conflict; if points of honor and of national pride like those here presented can be satisfactorily met without the shedding of innocent human blood, then surely there is no limit to what may be hoped for in the century that is to come. The United States has sedulously followed the earnest injunction of Washington in maintaining friendly relations with all nations while entering into alliance with none. Having been itself carved by revolution from the side of the British Empire, it is but natural that both the bonds of friendship and the causes for jealousy should be more numerous between the United States and the British Empire than between the United States and any other people. This is a plain historical fact which must be accepted by those who guide opinion and who frame public policies.

Friendship, close intercourse, and peace between the English-speaking peoples involve no antagonism to the interests or influence of

other nations. On the contrary, they are but
the beginning of a new world order when neither
differences of speech, nor of race, nor of creed
shall longer be permitted to sow dissension
among civilized men, or to arouse human passion to an extent where human reason cannot
control it and direct it toward the goal of justice, of human sympathy, and of a peace which
is lasting because it rests upon a secure economic and ethical foundation.

NICHOLAS MURRAY BUTLER.

COLUMBIA UNIVERSITY,
    *June* 4, 1914.

# CONTENTS

## CHAPTER I

PAGE

xi

xii                          CONTENTS

## CHAPTER IV

## CHAPTER V

## CHAPTER VI

## CHAPTER VII

## CHAPTER VIII

# INTRODUCTION

THAT the centenary of the treaty which has secured to Great Britain and the United States one hundred years of unbroken peace should deserve a celebration might seem strange to some philosopher in his study, whose meditations on the folly and cruelty of war would have led him to suppose that peace was natural between two great nations kindred in blood, both highly intelligent and highly civilized. Very different are the feelings of the historian, who remembers how often wars have arisen from slight causes, or of the practical statesman, who knows the kind of motives by which rulers who determine the issues of peace or war have been and still are governed. Jealousies, rivalries, antagonisms have still so much power over peoples, rulers are still so far from trying to apply as between states that moral law which the better sort of individual men recognize in private social and in business intercourse, and which public opinion imposes even upon the worse sort, that the maintenance of peace be-

tween neighbor states through three generations of men is a novel and admirable thing, fit
to inspire joy and deserve commemoration.

The peoples of these two states were no doubt
of kindred blood. But the quarrels of kins-
folk are proverbially bitter, and between these
there were plenty of causes for quarrel. The
separation, begun in 1776, sealed by treaty in
1783, had been made by war, a long war, which
left angry feelings. The behavior of some of
the British forces, and especially of the Hessian
mercenaries, had exasperated colonial sentiment, while the harshness with which the revolutionary party among the Americans had
treated those of their fellow citizens who ad-
hered to the British Crown had sown the seeds
of more enduring anger, especially among those
United Empire Loyalists who when expelled
from the United States took refuge in Canada.
For many years afterward the offensively super-
cilious attitude of the English and the self-assert-
ive arrogance of the Americans made the average man in each people distasteful to the other,
and it was only the wisest and largest minds that
preached good understanding and good feeling.
These aversions did not die down till the Civil
War of 1861-5, with its display of courage and

high spirit on both sides, had brought Europeans to respect the American people, and had given that people itself new martial deeds to be proud of, deeds of a valor which had not been directed against the old country.

Besides these unpleasant memories there were also controversies over important material interests that emerged from time to time. The northeastern frontier of the United States where the State of Maine borders on New Brunswick and Lower Canada had been left uncertain by the treaty of 1783, and also by that of 1814, and as the country began to be settled the disputes over it became threatening. After this question had been disposed of by the Webster-Ashburton treaty of 1842 another boundary quarrel arose for the possession of the region then called Oregon. Each nation had a legal case, and for many months neither seemed likely to give way. Even after the treaty of 1846 had fixed the forty-ninth parallel of latitude as the frontier line all the way to the shores of the Pacific, the diplomatists of both countries were harassed by a dispute relating to the ownership of the island of San Juan in the Straits of Juan de Fuca, and after that dispute had been referred to the German Emperor, and determined by him in favor of the United States, a larger issue was raised over the frontier of Alaska and that newly colonized extreme northwestern region of Canada which we call the Yukon. This was disposed of by a joint commission in 1903. There still remained one small outstanding controversy about a tiny island, called Pope's Folly, and some fishing-grounds in Passamaquoddy Bay (a large inlet from the Bay of Fundy), through which the international boundary runs. In 1911 an agreement was drafted to refer it to arbitration. When the negotiators, feeling the absurdity of employing the elaborate machinery of a court to determine so trivial a matter, agreed to split the difference, they gave the islet to the State of Maine while the fishing-grounds were assigned to the Canadian province of New Brunswick. With this there ended the long series of frontier questions that had so often been a source of disquiet, and now every yard of the nearly four thousand miles of boundary has been marked out by scientific surveyors. To have escaped or amicably settled all the grounds of friction which might occur along this line, far longer than any other frontier between civilized nations, is itself an event without parallel in history.

Even after the land boundary had been determined, the sea and the creatures that make the value of the sea remained to disturb the repose of the two nations. In the wandering waves one can fix no boundaries, and in the wandering fish one can assert no property, so fishing questions have always been a source of trouble. Questions arose regarding the seal fisheries of the Pacific. Controversies far more intricate and far more protracted produced an almost incessant irritation between the fishermen who came from New England to the coasts of Nova Scotia and Newfoundland and the native fishermen who plied their trade there under the British flag. Not till 1910 was this seemingly endless dispute adjusted by the sentence of The Hague tribunal which both parties accepted without a murmur.

The two nations were akin in blood and speech, but a common speech carries with it one disadvantage. Each nation can read all the ill-natured things that are said about it in the other; and there are never wanting those who like to say ill-natured things, sometimes from a vanity which seeks to exalt itself by depressing others, sometimes from a wish to compel attention and produce an effect—for in literature, and especially in journalism, blame draws more notice than praise—sometimes from pure ill nature, the love of mischief for mischief's sake. Thus, of the many offensive words uttered on both sides when temper was up, a larger proportion reached the eyes and ears of the other than if they had spoken different tongues, and what was spitefully said proved more galling.

There was, moreover, one exception to that community of ideas and traditions which was fitted to draw Americans and Englishmen together. From the third decade of the nineteenth century there had been a considerable immigration from Ireland to the United States. It increased largely after 1845, but it did not begin to be politically significant till the days of the Fenian movement, when some violent members of the insurrectionary party escaped to the United States and placed there their base of operations against the British Government. At the same time they sought to organize and to rouse the Irishmen settled in America, a large and rapidly growing element, against England. Not only the volume of the Irish vote but its compactness, as well as the prominence of Irish leaders in municipal government and in the party machine, made the constant attacks upon

England and the constant pressure upon Congressmen and on successive administrations to adopt an anti-British policy, a factor of some moment. After the remarkable change of British policy toward Ireland which began with Mr. Gladstone's Church Disestablishment Bill of 1869, and reached its high-water mark in his Home Rule Bill of 1886, this anti-English sentiment gradually declined, affecting an always diminishing percentage of that part of the American population which springs from an Irish stock and cherishes an Irish patriotism. It is now confined to a comparatively small section, and is likely soon to disappear. But from the end of the Civil War till about the end of the century it was an obstacle to perfectly good relations, being one of the many ways which Irishmen have found of avenging the wrongs their forefathers suffered at the hands of English governments.

Nevertheless, despite these grounds of dissension and others which need not be here recounted, peace did last unbroken, and, though there were several strains, none came quite to the breaking-point. The times at which the risk of a breach was greatest seem to have been the dispute about Oregon in 1845, the *Trent* affair in 1861, and the years just after the Civil War (1865 to 1871), when the resentment over the depredations committed by the *Alabama* was acute. The Venezuela incident at the end of 1895 was a passing squall, which the English, astonished at the vehemence shown over a matter which not one Englishman in a hundred had ever heard of, could not be induced to take seriously. In the two former of these instances there was some bellicose sentiment on both sides of the Atlantic, in the two latter such a sentiment existed on the American side only, and few persons in England could imagine war as likely to result.

To what causes, then, do we owe it that all the sources of trouble which from time to time arose, some of which were for the moment formidable, have so passed away that for more than a generation there has been a growing sense of concord and good will?

The cause which naturally occurs to most minds is blood kinship and a common speech. It is, however, easy to overrate the value of such a tie. It has not prevented fierce wars between communities of the same nationality. Athenians and Thebans bore to one another an undying hate. So did Pisans and Florentines. Bitter were the wars between German principalities in the sixteenth and seventeenth centuries. Tocqueville said in 1830 that he could conceive of no hatred more poisonous than that which the Americans then felt for England.[1] Kinship alone would not have been enough. Kinship, however, was reinforced by a sense of the common possession of a great literature and great traditions. The New Englanders, bitter as they often were toward England, could not forget that Milton and Cromwell were Englishmen. Many a Virginian family was proud of its Cavalier ancestry. So too, though it was at one time the fashion among the English upper and literary class to treat the Americans as a purely commercial people, and to disparage their literature, each nation had a genuine interest in the other's performances and a capacity for understanding the other which neither possessed as toward any other people. Each was secretly proud of the other, though neither would avow it. The American masses would from 1814 down to 1871 have felt less repulsion from the notion of armed strife than would the English, but fortu-

[1] One may, however, conjecture that in listening to the sharp words of his New England friends he underrated an underlying sentiment running the other way.

nately there was no standing army in the United States, and only a small navy, so that the country was free from that pernicious influence of a professional military caste which works such frightful evil in Europe, being indeed driven to desire opportunities for practising the work for which the profession exists. In Britain the army and navy never wished to fight America. They would have felt wars with her to be almost civil wars, *bella nullos habitura triumphos*. And when in recent years America began to have a great navy, her officers and sailors, as often as they found themselves in foreign ports, always fraternized with those of British vessels, and found the latter friends ready made.

The basis for good will grew wider and firmer with the increased intercourse of private citizens which followed the introduction of steam navigation. Private friendships became incomparably more numerous, and the interests of commerce were more closely interwoven.

Neither nation was drawn into war by such alliances with any other state as we now see to be among the most deadly sources of war. Happily for herself, America has had no entangling alliances; that risk existed only in 1793-5. Britain, not always so carefully detached, never has had, and it may safely be said never will have, any that could require her to array herself against America.

But the main factor working for peace has been the good sense and self-control inherent in the character of the two peoples. Neither of them suffers itself to be swept away by passion, neither forgets, even when demagogues seek to excite it by appeals to national vanity and so-called "points of honor," that there are, behind the susceptibilities of the moment, large issues of permanent well-being to be considered. In the days when both nations claimed Oregon, a territory of great extent and value, imperfectly as that value was then known, was in dispute. But in both countries public opinion recognized that the other side also had a case, and that war would be a greater evil than the loss of part of its own rights. The territory was accordingly divided and peace was preserved. So on other occasions also the peoples came near the brink of a rupture, but showed their inborn quality by stopping on the brink.

The question arises—and it is a question of high interest—how much of this self-restraint and underlying wisdom is to be attributed to the fact that the United States Government ever

since 1814 and the British Government ever
since 1832 have been popular governments, in
which the general feeling of the nation has been,
though more evidently in the United States than
in Britain, the ultimately decisive factor in
international relations. One would like to as-
cribe much weight to this factor, for it would be
reassuring as to the pacific tendencies of democracies in general. But the facts are not all one
way. Let us consider them. It is clear that
if the government of Britain had been as popular in 1776 as it was in 1876 the North American colonies would not have been alienated as
they unhappily were, and also clear that in 1862
the existence of a wide-spread sympathy for the
Northern States among the British masses immensely diminished the risk that the British
Government might yield to the persuasions of
the French Emperor and might thus, in recognizing the independence of the Southern Confederacy, find herself in a conflict with the
North.[1] But on every occasion since 1814 in

[1] A well-known writer, General von Bernhardi, observes in his recent
book, *Germany and the Next War* (p. 94 of English translation): "England
committed the unpardonable blunder, from her point of view, of not
supporting the Southern States in the American War of Secession."
What the Prussian general calls an "unpardonable blunder" was the
scornful refusal of the British nation—a practically unanimous refusal—
to take advantage of the divisions in a kindred people and set back the
cause of human freedom.

which peace seemed to be threatened from the American side, popular feeling in the United States was, or seemed to be, so far bellicose that the statesmen who directed American policy thought they could make political capital out of a menacing attitude. Such was the case with Mr. Polk and Mr. Seward, and again with Mr. Blaine; and such seemed to be the case with Mr. Cleveland in December, 1895, though the motives with which he launched his message of that year have never been fully understood. If nothing similar happened in Britain, it must be remembered that the questions which arose between the two countries were all (except the *Trent* affair) remote from the knowledge and interest of the great bulk of Englishmen, so that it was never worth the while of any politician, however free from scruples, to win any popular favor by an anti-American policy. Had the controversies which arose over Canadian issues directly affected Britain, or, in other words, had the English been Canadians, defending their view of their rights to disputed territory or to absolute control of sea-fisheries, the temper of the British people might have been more sensitive and their latent pugnacity more easily aroused.

One remarkable proof of good feeling and of a good sense which rises to the level of the highest political wisdom has been of late years given by the people of the United States. There was a time when they desired to complete their control of the North American continent by absorbing Canada. It was a natural desire, for there were geographical considerations which seemed to favor it, and it would, if peaceably effected, have increased their strength and wealth. But never since 1814 have they seriously thought of using force against Canada, for they know that just governments are based on the consent of the governed, while in recent years they have frankly renounced the notion of employing any kind even of a pacific pressure, and have recognized in a large-minded and friendly spirit that Canada has a patriotic ideal of her own and wishes both to become a great nation and to maintain her political connection with the mother-country and those other great dominions which regard the ancient crown of Britain as their centre of unity. In this matter at least let us stop to honor and admire the spirit of American democracy.

He who reads this record which Professor

Dunning has set forth with so much judgment as
well as with a conspicuous impartiality, will be
struck by the fact that groundless suspicions
by either nation of the purposes of the other,
and the attribution by either to the other of
motives which did not exist or were of slight
importance, played no small part in the imbit-
terment of relations.  Such suspicions and mis-
conceptions between states are always to be
feared.  They have been fruitful sources of
strife.  That they did not, as between Britain
and America, prove fatal in times of strain may
be ascribed to the fact that there were always
in both nations men capable of correcting these
misapprehensions, and that each knew enough
of its own defects to be able to make al-
lowances for the like defects in the other.  The
most serious misapprehension was that which,
owing largely to the unwisdom of a section of
the English press, arose during the Civil War,
when most Americans supposed that a jealous
spirit made England desire the downfall of the
Republic.  That was never the case, as I can
venture to assert from my recollection of those
now distant days.  There was a good deal of
sympathy with the valor and constancy of the
Confederates.  But the fact was, though Amer-

icans did not then know it, that the bulk of the British people, and most of its intellectual leaders, men like John Bright and Goldwin Smith, always stood for the cause which they held to be that of human rights and of democratic progress. During the years from 1861 to 1865 no meetings open to the general public were (so far as I can remember) ever held to give support to the Confederate cause, because it was known that in such an open meeting no resolution adverse to the North could have been carried on a vote. In the upper classes there were then some people who would have liked to see a republic discredited. But the larger heart of the British nation as a whole refused the most favorable opportunity it ever had of injuring its greatest competitor.

Though Professor Dunning is right in dwelling upon the fact that the gradual democratization of Britain tended to the promotion of good relations, it is to be noted that in neither country was either of the great parties identified with either an anti-American or an anti-British tendency. Party politics came but little into the matter. But men, that is to say, the views and characters of individual statesmen, did come in, and made an immense difference.

The portraits of Webster and Ashburton that hang on the walls of the State Department at Washington commemorate two negotiators whose happy co-operation solved a problem the solution of which might, in the hands of lesser men, have been remitted to the sword. On that occasion both the United States and Canada were displeased, the press of each declaring that its representative had conceded far too much. That has almost always been said in both countries alike when any compromise was made. But the outer world and posterity have approved the compromise. Neither American nor British interests were always in the keeping of men so tactful and prudent as Webster and Ashburton. There were moments when the stiff and frigid attitude of the British foreign secretary exasperated the American negotiators, or when a demagogic secretary of state at Washington tried by a bullying tone to win credit as the patriotic champion of national claims. But whenever there were bad manners in London there was good temper at Washington, and when there was a storm on the Potomac there was calm on the Thames. It was the good fortune of the two countries that if at any moment rashness or vehemence was found on one side, it never happened to be met by the like quality on the other.

The moral of the story which Professor Dunning has told so clearly is that peace can always be kept, whatever be the grounds of controversy, between peoples that wish to keep it. Mr. Root, the greatest of Webster's successors in the office of secretary of state, has well said that there is no issue in diplomacy which cannot be settled if the negotiators sincerely try to settle it. The questions that arose between these two countries were questions in which, especially on the American side, the negotiators could not act without having the mind and will of the people behind them, because the people had some knowledge of the questions, a knowledge far wider than European nations have of the controversies that arise between their governments. The people could exert their judgment, and their judgment, even in moments of excitement, realized how frightful would be the calamities of a fratricidal war.

This feeling has grown immensely stronger within the last half-century, as any one whose recollection extends that far back can testify. It is a guarantee of unbroken peace for the future. May not that sense of an unbreakable

peace have effects going beyond the two nations whom it blesses? They understand one
another. The material interests that unite them
are greater than ever before, the private friendships more numerous, the reciprocal knowledge
of one another more complete. Are they not
naturally fitted to act together whenever their
efforts can be jointly put forth on behalf of
international justice and peace, confirming by
their influence the good which their example
has already done? They have given the finest
example ever seen in history of an undefended
frontier, along which each people has trusted
to the good faith of the other that it would
create no naval armaments; and this very
absence of armaments has itself helped to prevent hostile demonstrations. Neither of them
has ever questioned the sanctity of treaties,
or denied that states are bound by the moral
law.

Be that as it may, it is, to those who are sad-
dened by the calamities which the year 1914
has brought upon Europe, a consoling thought
that the century of peace which has raised the
English-speaking peoples from forty millions
to one hundred and sixty millions has created
among those peoples a sense of kindliness and

good will which was never seen before, and which is the surest pledge of their future prosperity and progress, as well as of the maintenance of a Perpetual Friendship between them.

JAMES BRYCE.

HINDLEAP, SUSSEX,
*September* 14, 1914.

# THE BRITISH EMPIRE
### AND
# THE UNITED STATES

## CHAPTER I

### READJUSTMENT AFTER WAR

In the late afternoon of December 24, 1814, the commissioners who had agreed upon the Treaty of Ghent signed their handiwork and exchanged conventional expressions of satisfaction at the conclusion of their labors. John Quincy Adams, as he tells us in his diary, assured Lord Gambier of his hope that it would be the last treaty of peace between Great Britain and the United States. Two weeks later, at a banquet given by the citizens in honor of the commissioners, Mr. Adams, proposing the culminating toast of the occasion, worded it thus: "Ghent, the city of Peace; may the gates of the temple of Janus, here closed, not be opened again for a century!"

It is not likely that a conscientious search of his heart, such as Mr. Adams was wont to engage in at times, would have revealed any very large measure of the confidence that his formal words had implied. Neither in the course of the negotiations nor in their result could the most sanguine observer have found assurance of even the lesser degree of permanence that had been piously suggested. Actual war between English-speaking peoples the treaty did indeed bring to an end; the causes of the war it did not make the subject of even a remote allusion.

By all the canons of judgment that were warranted by history and by the conditions of the times, the peace made at Ghent could be merely a truce. Great Britain in 1815 stood on the pinnacle of fame as the mightiest political power on earth. Her population of 19,000,000 was not large, relatively speaking, but it was compact. Included in it were some 5,000,000 Irishmen, who, though perpetually troublesome in some respects, could always be depended upon to furnish a goodly quota of both brains and brawn in war. Her navy had established an undisputed control of all the seas. Her army, under Wellington, had given the final blow to the prestige of the greatest military genius of modern times, if not of all times. Her colonial possessions, largely increased by the twenty years of war just ended, covered vast areas in every part of the globe. Commercially, no other power approached her in the magnitude of her interests. In manufactures she was slowly but surely forging to the front on lines that were soon to revolutionize industry. Politically and socially the forces that made up this mighty organism were centred in a narrow aristocracy. The landowners of the United Kingdom ruled the British Empire. There was indeed a monarch; there was a House of Commons; there were courts and juries and bills of rights and all the elements that had for centuries been the vaunted guarantees of English liberty. In the actual working of the complex system, however, the decisive influence was wielded by the landed aristocracy, and more particularly by the peers whose estates constituted so significant a fraction of the surface of the islands.

The United States, when it ventured to engage in war with this huge empire, presented a contrast with its adversary that was almost ludicrous. A population of 8,000,000, of whom some 1,500,000 were negro slaves, was scattered along a thousand miles of the Atlantic seaboard, with a few straggling lines of settlement in the Mississippi valley. For military power this nation could boast a dozen half-filled regiments of regular troops, distributed in small detachments over the whole territory, and a navy so insignificant in size as to evoke roars of laughter when the number of its ships was mentioned in the House of Commons. Before the end of the war this minute navy had given such an account of itself as no longer to be a cause of mirth at Westminster, and even the army, after bitter humiliation, had won somewhat of distinction. Yet in no sense could the United States be reckoned as of much significance among the powers of the civilized world. Its foreign commerce had assumed some importance during the long Napoleonic wars, but could expect no great development in the competition with Great Britain after peace had been made. In manufacturing, a little impetus had been given by the exclusion of British goods through embargo and war; but here again the restoration of peace would put the Americans under the crushing weight of competition from England and would end, for the time at least, any likelihood that the United States would figure among the important industrial powers.

The one aspect in which the American Republic attracted serious attention among enlightened nations was the political and social. Here was to be found in practical operation on a large scale the democracy that the French Revolution had threatened to impose upon all Europe. Liberty and equality of a kind and degree portentously suggestive of the ideals of 1789 and 1792 prevailed throughout the United States and were watched with some anxiety by the dominant classes in the Old World. It was a cardinal maxim of conservative political philosophy in Europe that republican government could not be adapted to the needs of a great territory and population. The career of the American Republic was expected therefore to be stormy and brief. War with the United States in 1812 had not been desired by the British governing aristocracy; it involved an annoying diversion of attention and resources from the serious business of the hour. Only because it might in some measure hasten the inevitable failure and downfall of the American system was it regarded with any equanimity. The attitude of the New England Federalists during hostilities had confirmed this feeling in the class among whom it prevailed, and the feeling was manifest in the negotiations by which the war was brought to an end.

It would indeed be a serious error to assume that the feeling here referred to was very general in England. Party divisions, though dimmed by the national solidarity that was developed by the exigencies of the long war with France, still marked the line of cleavage in political thinking, and the Whigs, for decades in a hopeless opposition, still bore the tradition of admiration and pride concerning the branch of the English race which Tory policy had severed from the parent stem. Conspicuous features of American constitutional practice were the goal of Whig aspiration and this fact tended to produce tolerance of other features that were abhorrent. Thoroughgoing democracy such as was manifest in the United States was no more attractive to the Whigs than to the Tories. The Tories, however, feared it, while the Whigs looked indulgently upon it as a pathetic error that would in time correct itself. To the Tory the American people was a brawling, disreputable loafer, who had disgraced his family by plundering it and had by his character and conduct put himself beyond the possibility of toleration by any member of respectable society.  The Whig, on the other hand, felt toward the United States much as the upper-class college man feels toward the freshman, the journeyman toward the apprentice, the old and sophisticated in any occupation toward the newcomer.  The strong points of the new man were duly appreciated and admired; there was satisfaction that the English-speaking group should include a stout, smart, likely young fellow, and there was shrewd calculation of what he could contribute in a competition or fight with a rival group; but there was a feeling that within his own group he must learn his place and keep it, and must submit peaceably to the hazing and fagging that were the prerogative of his elders.

It was the Tory point of view that dominated the British approach to the negotiations at Ghent.  For their temerity in undertaking the conquest of Canada the Americans must be required to surrender enough territory to make a renewal of that enterprise very difficult; and, moreover, they must refrain from all discussion of the practice of search and impressment, which they held to be the cause of the war.

The announcement of these terms by the British commissioners at Ghent suspended negotiation abruptly. Peace on any terms involving cession of territory by the United States was promptly shown by the attitude of the Americans to be impossible; the Britons at the same time were unyielding as to search and impressment. Accordingly, peace pure and simple was agreed to. The Treaty of Ghent embodied, in addition to the articles necessary to end the war, only certain provisions for determining the northern boundary of the United States as fixed by the treaty of 1783, and an agreement to promote the abolition of the slave trade. Matters of grave and pressing importance, the right of search, the navigation of the Mississippi and the Saint Lawrence Rivers, the rights of inshore fishing on the Atlantic coast—all were broached, but were dropped from consideration in order to insure the one great end of peace.

In the United States peace was greeted with universal rejoicing. The chagrin of those in authority at the failure of a far-reaching settlement found no place in popular feeling. In the dazzling glamour of McDonough's victory on Lake Champlain and Jackson's final achievement at New Orleans, the humiliation of Detroit and Washington and Chrystler's Farm was lost to sight entirely, and the belief hardened into century-long tradition that in a second war for independence the Americans had won as decisive a triumph as that which was crowned at Yorktown.

In Great Britain, meanwhile, the conclusion of peace with the United States was scarcely noted, and the very fact that there had been a war was forgotten. The news that the Treaty of Ghent had been ratified reached London almost simultaneously with the report that Napoleon had returned from Elba. Already for months the progress of affairs at the Congress of Vienna had enlisted the anxious attention of all Europe. Lord Castlereagh, the British foreign secretary, on his way to Vienna with a train of twenty coaches, as John Quincy Adams casually noted, had stopped at Ghent long enough, in August, 1814, to give the British negotiators the instructions that made the conclusion of the treaty possible. The conflicting interests and cross-purposes that were in play at Vienna had made a renewal of widespread war among the great European powers not unlikely; the astonishing reception of Napoleon in France made it practically certain.

In the presence of such a prospect it was not to be expected that the petty affair of American relations should excite any interest. Then followed the Hundred Days, Waterloo, and Saint Helena. These furnished engrossing material for British reflection, both popular and official, and all things American faded from view and from memory.

No such oblivion enveloped the recent events in that group of loyal Britons who dwelt in the provinces north of the United States. Of the half-million inhabitants of these provinces some fifty per cent were English-speaking, and of this fifty per cent the most influential element consisted of the families who had been driven from the United States by the result of the Revolution. New Brunswick and Upper Canada were peopled almost exclusively by these exiles. In them the memories and traditions of the civil strife that had caused them such hardships nourished undying bitterness toward the Americans. Toward the thriving democracy to the south the attitude of the British Canadian was that of the English Tory. When war broke out in 1812, with the loudly proclaimed purpose of Henry Clay and other sanguine spirits to sweep over Canada and dictate

peace at Quebec or Halifax, both French and
British subjects rallied faithfully to the colors
of the King, but there was a special ardor in
the response of the British. Those who recalled
the proceedings of the triumphant party in New
York and other States at the end of the Revolutionary War could not be lured to welcome
the invaders by any call to escape from oppression. It happened that the brunt of the fighting on land fell upon the scattered communities
of Upper Canada, where anti-American feeling
was strongest, and the loss and suffering inevitable in even minor hostilities were greatest
along the shores of Lakes Erie and Ontario and
the marvellous river that connects them. This
region, destined to become the leading province
of the British dominion in America, was permeated thus with the stories of heroic effort,
sacrifice, and triumph in resistance to invasion.
To the original Loyalist hatred of the American
Republic was thus added the confirming force
of a patriotic tradition, and no little impulse
was given to the influence that was working to
develop a proud and prosperous English-speaking state on the northern half of the continent.

That the hope and wish for such a future development were less prevalent in England than

among the Loyalists in Canada is manifest in a remark of Alexander Baring (later Lord Ashburton) to John Quincy Adams in 1816: ". . . it is in vain for us to think of growing strong there [in Canada] in the same proportion as America. . . . He wished the British government would give us Canada at once. It . . . was fit for nothing but to breed quarrels." Baring's pessimistic observation was made in the course of a conversation on the question of disarmament on the Great Lakes, and was premonitory of a feeling among British publicists that was to become wide-spread and notorious by the middle of the century. At the time when Baring's private opinion was revealed and was recorded with grim satisfaction by Adams, the feeling that gave rise to it was probably shared by very few leaders of British policy. Yet the events of the war had served to give the officials of the Colonial Department much uneasiness about the exposed condition of Upper Canada and had thus led to the demand for territorial readjustments that should bar the Americans from the shores of Lakes Erie, Huron, and Superior. The demand was peremptorily rejected, but the purpose behind it remained active. When, therefore, the peace had been made and the British Government had sufficiently recovered from its Napoleonic distractions to give some attention to American affairs, it came to pass, happily enough, that the situation on the frontier of Upper Canada was the first of the many disturbing questions at issue that was satisfactorily adjusted by diplomacy.

The work of the diplomats on the problems left unsettled by both the war and the treaty of peace was begun in the middle of 1815, with the negotiation of a convention of commerce and navigation at London. John Quincy Adams, Clay, and Gallatin wrestled again with the Britons who had been at Ghent, but made no progress toward securing for the United States the eagerly sought privileges of trade with the British-American colonies. The treaty signified practically nothing beyond the formal resumption of reciprocal commerce as it had existed before the war, the East Indies becoming again the only transmarine dependencies of Great Britain with which American vessels were permitted to carry on trade.

The matter of the armaments on the Great Lakes was formally entered upon diplomatically only at the beginning of 1816. Under instruc-

tions from Washington, John Quincy Adams,
now minister of the United States at London,
proposed to Lord Castlereagh that both governments set a limit to their respective naval
forces on the Lakes. The actual situation there
had given much concern to American and British authorities alike. The termination of hostilities came in the midst of energetic efforts by
the commanders on both sides of the frontier
to complete and equip new and larger vessels.
Especially on Lake Ontario, where the superiority of the Americans was less clearly established than elsewhere, the rivalry in naval construction was most energetic and ambitious.
The primitive processes by which a few acres
of forest had been turned almost overnight
into fleets of small but sufficient war-ships were
now being developed and extended to more
pretentious designs. At Kingston, on the Canadian side, Sir James Yeo was pressing toward completion one ship-of-the-line that should
mount 110 guns and two that should mount
74, and across the lake at Sacketts Harbor two
rival 74's were on the stocks. Many lesser
craft were in various stages of construction.
The cessation of hostilities naturally did not
end the strenuous rivalry. The same reason-

ing that was destined a century later to fill the oceans and the scrap-heaps of all the world with gigantic masses of steel, operated to keep at full tension the workers on the puny wooden structures that embodied the hope of triumphant sea-power in the earlier day. Only when the actual strain on the finances of the governments overcame the care for a contingent future of naval glory, was a halt called in the extravagant proceedings on the Lakes.

The proposition of Adams for disarmament met with no satisfactory response at first from Lord Castlereagh. His Lordship freely admitted the ruinous consequences that were threatened by the competition in fleet-building, but urged that, because Great Britain was at a great disadvantage as compared with the United States in respect to facilities for defensive equipment in that remote region, any restriction of force should apply to the Americans only. The truth was that the British cabinet were seriously divided on the policy to be pursued in this matter. A party headed by Lord Bathurst, the colonial secretary, insisted that an overwhelming naval force should be created on the Lakes, so as to render forever out of the question any American aggression upon Upper

Canada.  Demands for this policy were strongly
urged in both Parliament and the press during
the winter and spring of 1816, and gave Adams
much anxiety.  Ultimately, however, the belligerent faction was overcome by the pacifists
of the government, and Adams, much to his
surprise, was informed by Castlereagh in April
that the proposal for disarmament would be
taken up for discussion.

The detailed discussion of the business was
transferred to Washington, where it was handled
by Monroe, the secretary of state, and Bagot,
the British minister.  Final action was not
reached without considerable delay.  On both
sides of the water there prevailed in military
and naval circles, and was reflected in the press,
the usual post-bellum irritation and bluster,
making the diplomats cautious.  Adams reported his fear that the sudden change in
Castlereagh's attitude concealed some treachery, and Bagot was suspicious of an ulterior
motive behind Monroe's earnestness in seeking
a settlement.  All the clouds were dissipated,
however, and at the end of April, 1817, a
formal agreement was effected by an exchange
of notes at Washington.  By this date Monroe
had become President of the United States, and

the State Department was under the charge of Richard Rush, pending the return from abroad of the new secretary, John Quincy Adams. The notes were signed, therefore, by Rush and Bagot respectively, and the arrangement embodied in them became known as the Rush-Bagot Agreement. By its terms each government bound itself to limit its naval force on the frontier to four vessels, each not exceeding one hundred tons burthen and armed with one 18-pound cannon, one vessel to be stationed on Lake Ontario, two on the Upper Lakes, and one on Lake Champlain. All other war-ships on these lakes were to be forthwith dismantled, and no others were to be there built or armed.

In conformity with this arrangement the British authorities disposed of their three ships-of-the-line, six medium-sized vessels, and many smaller craft, while the Americans dismantled, sold, or scuttled and sank a number considerably larger. So long as the good faith of the two governments endured, it was thus insured that the Great Lakes should be free from the martial ardor that is inevitably inspired by the parade of rival forces. The future was to show that even more important than this direct influence was the indirect effect of the adjustment in setting the standard of peaceful methods for the determination of the vexatious problems that arose along the whole long boundary between the United States and British America.

The comprehensive consideration of the questions at issue between the United States and Great Britain in connection with the late war was taken up in 1817 at London. Two years of general peace had by this time cleared up many cloudy matters of domestic and foreign politics and the British cabinet could devote some leisurely attention to the issues which the Americans were so insistent on bringing forward for settlement. It could not be said that the slow progress toward a settlement was due to any ill feeling on the part of the British Government toward the United States. So far as Castlereagh's conduct at the Foreign Office was concerned, not even John Quincy Adams, temperamentally indisposed to approval of an adversary, could find much to criticise, while Richard Rush, who in 1817 succeeded Adams as minister at London, positively and warmly proclaimed the conciliatory disposition of the secretary. Charles Bagot was sent to Washington with imperative instructions to promote cordial relations with the American Government, and his success in accomplishing this was understood to be the condition of his future advancement in his diplomatic career. He did not anticipate much pleasure from his task. He was an intimate of George Canning, whose antipathy to Castlereagh and all his works made much scandal in the circles of the ruling aristocracy. "Your plan of treatment," wrote Canning to Bagot just after his appointment in 1815, "may or may not succeed with the Yankees, but it is obviously, for your sake, the proper one. I am afraid, indeed, that the question is not so much how you will treat them as how they will treat you, and that the hardest lesson which a British Minister has to learn in America is not what to do, but what to bear. But even this may come round. And Waterloo is a great help to you, perhaps a necessary help after the (to say the least) balanced successes and misfortunes of the American war."

Despite all the obstacles, however, Bagot succeeded in his undertaking. Though he was fully impressed with the fact that ill feeling toward Great Britain was a controlling influence in the predominant party in the country, he was tactful and far-sighted enough to establish at Washington the same official cordiality that

Rush reported at London. Under such favorable conditions the negotiations that were intended to define the results of the war proceeded to a conclusion in the treaty that was signed at London October 20, 1818.

This convention fell far short of what the Americans had hoped for. Its omissions were almost as significant as those of the Treaty of Ghent. In particular, there was no reference to the right of search and impressment. This subject had naturally been put first in importance of the long list on which Rush was instructed to seek an agreement. His efforts revealed at the very outset, so far as the fundamental principle at issue was concerned, the same hopeless *impasse* that had existed for twenty years. Great Britain stood absolutely immovable on her right to search foreign merchantmen on the high seas for British seamen; the United States declared categorically that she would never admit the right of any foreigner to muster the crew of an American vessel on their own ship. In view of this unpromising antagonism on fundamental principle, the negotiations made a degree of progress that was highly significant of the conciliatory spirit on both sides. Castlereagh freely conceded that

the practice of visitation and search by the
British commanders had been attended with
serious abuses, and he was ready to do everything possible to prevent their recurrence.
Rush ultimately agreed that the best way to
attain this end was to keep British seamen out
of American ships. Accordingly, a draft treaty
was actually formulated in which Great Britain
abandoned the visitation of American ships except for purposes recognized by both governments as justifiable by international law, while
the United States undertook to exclude from
service in its merchant marine all natural-born
subjects of Great Britain, even those who
should in the future become American citizens
under the naturalization laws.

This project eventually was dropped, on account of disagreements on subsidiary points
concerning ratification and administration. It
probably involved rather too large concessions
for the time and circumstances on both sides.
America had already become as tenacious of
her claim concerning the rights of her naturalized citizens as Britain was concerning the
right of her navy to recruit its forces wherever
it could find British seamen. The points on
which the treaty came to grief were so rela-

tively insignificant as strongly to suggest that they were merely a cover for retreat from a too advanced position on the main questions. Whatever was the truth in this matter, the failure of the project left active a serious menace to the peace of the two nations. The peril was destined to endure until the progress of ideas had undermined the British conviction that the brutal practice of impressment was the only adequate means by which to insure naval pre-eminence, and until the growth and prestige of the United States had made respect for her claims as to the rights of her citizens a necessity in practice if not in theory.

Of the subjects on which agreement was actually embodied in the convention of 1818, the majority involved relations between the United States and the British possessions to the north of it. Most important was the adjustment of the differences as to the fisheries on the Atlantic coast. By the treaty of peace in 1783 Great Britain recognized the right of the people of the United States to take fish on the banks of Newfoundland, in the Gulf of Saint Lawrence, and at sea in general, and further accorded the "liberty" of fishing on practically all the coasts, bays, and creeks of

British America, with the additional "liberty"
of drying and curing fish on certain unsettled
parts of the shore. By these provisions a prominent American industry was made very prosperous and profitable. The excessive generos-
ity of the British negotiators was severely
criticised by their compatriots on both sides of
the Atlantic. At Ghent, in 1814, there was an
opportunity to correct the error of the earlier
treaty. Accordingly, the British commissioners took the position that, under a familiar
principle of international law, the fisheries
article of 1783, like all the rest of that convention, had been abrogated by war between the
signatory governments. The Americans were
fully equipped with reasons why this principle
did not apply to the fisheries article. The
debate reached no conclusion, however, on account of the agreement to treat of peace only.

After hostilities ceased friction naturally arose
in the fishing regions. The Americans resumed
their accustomed pursuit of the herring and cod
in the accustomed places; the British authorities in the Maritime Provinces manifested a
purpose to protect their coast from the intrusion of the Americans. A zealous naval commander even warned an American fisherman

who was plying his vocation out of sight of land not to venture to do so within sixty miles of the shore. Protests on these incidents evoked from the British Foreign Office at last the formal declaration that it claimed no right to interfere with fishing on the high sea, but that it would treat as extinct the liberty once recognized to Americans to take and cure fish on any British coasts or bays. It was obviously high time for serious effort to remove so disagreeable a situation as was thus created.

In the negotiations on the subject the case of the Americans was almost hopeless. The inshore privileges long enjoyed were vital to the prosperity of a great industry that centred in Massachusetts. To maintain these privileges, however, it was necessary to sustain two contentions that were desperately weak, namely, that the "liberty" accorded by the treaty of 1783 was in reality a right under the law of nature and of nations, and that this liberty or right had not been abrogated by the war. Gallatin and Rush, the American plenipotentiaries, as well as Secretary Adams, who directed them, were adepts in the diplomatist's art of extracting from the hazy realms of nature and history the particular principle or precedent that happened to be useful to their cause; but their skill availed little against the stiff British dogma that territorial jurisdiction was absolute as against the claims of any foreign power, especially one that had recently failed of success in war.

The result, however, in the actual treaty provisions was more favorable to the American interests than had *prima facie* seemed possible. Great Britain again made substantial concessions. The liberty of inshore fishing was assured forever to the inhabitants of the United States on certain limited stretches of British coast, namely, in Newfoundland, the whole western shore and an important piece of the southern; in Labrador, from a designated point in the Gulf of Saint Lawrence eastward and northward indefinitely; and all the shores of the Magdalen Islands. In Labrador and the south of Newfoundland drying and curing fish on shore was also permitted. Besides the solid gain contained in these provisions, the American commissioners flattered themselves that they had saved their face in the very terms in which the fishing privileges were abandoned as to all the other British coasts. "And the United States hereby renounce forever any liberty heretofore enjoyed or claimed" as to fishing within three miles of coasts, bays, creeks, or harbors outside of the foregoing limits. This wording was held to imply that the inshore privileges recognized in the treaty were not newly granted or ever *granted* by Great Britain, but were part of a natural heritage possessed by the United States, of which another and larger part was voluntarily renounced.

It is interesting to notice that, despite the meticulous care which the Americans devoted to the phrasing of the article, with a view to its more or less metaphysical implications, there remained in it the germ of a long and vexatious dispute on a most practical point of interpretation. Within twenty years of the signing of the treaty the British Government took the position that the "bays" from which the Americans were excluded embraced great expanses of deep sea where fishermen could ply their vocation on the largest scale without coming within three miles of the shore. If any one concerned in the negotiation of the treaty in 1818 suspected the possibility of such a view, he left no record of his insight.

In addition to the settlement as to the fisheries, this treaty dealt with the delimitation of territory from the Lake of the Woods to the Pacific Ocean. No serious controversy developed over this matter, not because the views of the two parties were entirely harmonious, but because the occupation of the vast wilderness concerned was as yet on too limited a scale to raise any immediate issue. From the Lake of the Woods to the summit of the Rocky Mountains it was easily agreed that the forty-ninth degree of latitude should be the boundary. As no one knew the position of the lake with reference to the parallel, but all felt sure that a meridian from the lake would cross the parallel somewhere, it was provided that from the northwestern point of the lake a north and south line should be run, if necessary, to intersect the parallel, and this line, with the parallel, should mark the boundary. West of the Rocky Mountains, however, the Oregon country, with its great rivers and its long and much indented Pacific coast, presented problems and possibilities of such obvious magnitude that neither party was especially eager to press for a definitive adjustment till fuller knowledge was forthcoming. Both British and American merchants had established fur-trading stations on the coast, and from the opposite direction

the Oregon country had been penetrated by
the hardy and enterprising agents of great commercial interests centring respectively at Saint
Louis and Montreal.  All that was provided
by the treaty was that the whole region, so far
as claimed by either Great Britain or the United
States, should for ten years be free and open to
the vessels, citizens, and subjects of the two
powers.

The most satisfactory feature of the convention of 1818, so far as concerned delimitation of
territory, was the provision by which a thousand miles of the boundary was made dependent
upon the fairly certain mechanical processes
of the surveyor.  An astronomical line will indeed vary with the personality of the men
and the precision of the instruments employed
in determining it, but it is certainty itself as
compared with most other customary means
of demarcation.  *A priori* one might suppose
that geographical features, such as rivers and
mountains, fixed by nature beyond the ordinary
power of man to change, would furnish the
most satisfactory boundaries.  Experience has
proved, however, that this is very far from the
truth.  Not until the present century, when
almost every mile of the thousands in North

America where British and American possessions are contiguous has been marked by monuments erected by human hands, have controversies over territorial limits been set finally
at rest.

At the time when the convention of 1818, by
the provision for the joint occupation of Oregon,
postponed a dangerous dispute concerning the
western side of the continent, a serious but
unsuccessful effort was in progress to adjust
a threatening difference at the far eastern end
of the line. The treaty of peace in 1783 had
been singularly unsuccessful in the attempt to
make clear the northern boundary of the United
States. Difficulties in running the line made
their appearance all the way from the Atlantic
Ocean to the Lake of the Woods. The start-
ing-point was set forth with much apparent
particularity in the treaty: "From the northwest angle of Nova Scotia, *viz.*, that angle
which is formed by a line drawn due north from
the source of Saint Croix River to the Highlands; along the Highlands which divide those
rivers which empty themselves into the river
Saint Lawrence, from those which fall into the
Atlantic Ocean, to the northwesternmost head
of Connecticut River . . ." But no one knew

or ever discovered the whereabouts of the "northwest angle of Nova Scotia"; the "Highlands" referred to could not be identified; the rivers "which fall into the Atlantic Ocean" might or might not include those that reached their destination by way of the great gulfs and bays that abounded in the neighborhood, and much depended on which alternative was selected; the "northwesternmost head of the Connecticut River" was doubtful and undetermined. Most important of all at the outset, moreover, was the fact that the two governments disagreed as to what stream was meant by the Saint Croix River. As the middle of this river, from mouth to source, completed, in the treaty, the long circuit of the boundary as there described, and separated Maine from New Brunswick, it early became imperative to settle on the identity of the Saint Croix. Only after fifteen years of controversy was an agreement reached. In 1798 a joint commission provided for in Jay's Treaty found that the Schoodic River was what the treaty meant by the Saint Croix, and determined by survey its mouth and its source.

This was the limit of the progress made prior to the War of 1812. In the Treaty of Ghent the boundary question was taken up in earnest, and three distinct commissions were provided for, with recourse to arbiters in case of disagreement between the commissioners.

The whole undetermined line from the Atlantic to the Lake of the Woods was parcelled out to these bodies for final survey and indication. Only one of the commissions was successful in its task: the course of the line among the islands in Passamaquoddy Bay and the Bay of Fundy was agreed upon without much trouble. At the other end of the boundary, between Lake Huron and the Lake of the Woods, some points were presented on which the commissioners could not reach an agreement, but no pressing necessity for a settlement arose. The task of the third commission, namely, to run the line from the head of the Saint Croix to the point where the Saint Lawrence is intersected by the forty-fifth parallel of north latitude, proved to be wholly beyond its power. The commissioners toiled for five years, from 1816 to 1821, only to reach a hopeless disagreement. As the "northwest angle of Nova Scotia" the opinions of the two commissioners designated respectively points that were 105 miles apart; their views as to the "highlands," etc., left a

region of over ten thousand square miles in dispute on the frontier of Maine and New Brunswick; and further the discovery was made, much
to the discomfort of the Americans, that what
had for fifty years passed for the forty-fifth
parallel and served as the boundary between
New York and Vermont on the one side and
Canada on the other, was in fact so far from the
true parallel as to leave on British soil a costly
fortress under construction by the United States
at Rouse's Point.

The progress of settlement and development
made this situation a cause of great concern to
the two governments. Arbitration was arranged in 1827 and the King of the Netherlands
was chosen as umpire. His opinion, pronounced
in 1831, frankly declared the impossibility of
deciding which, if either, of the conflicting
claims conformed to the terms of the treaty of
1783, and proposed a line that divided the
region in dispute. This proposal was not accepted by either government, and the matter
remained to be the source of ever-increasing
friction, as we shall see, until 1842.

If the character of their formal diplomatic
intercourse were a conclusive criterion of the
general feeling of two nations toward each other,

cordial respect and friendship would be said to have prevailed between Great Britain and the United States in the years immediately following the end of the war. Even when, as in regard to the right of search, differences of view were obstinate and irreconcilable, the debate had involved no display of bitterness. All the negotiations had been correct and amicable according to the most exacting requirements of the diplomatist's art. The technique of this art, however, consists largely in devices through which good manners shall cover feelings of quite another sort. A model plenipotentiary may be an indifferent index of the national spirit which he represents. Like the second in an affair of honor, he must guide his principal along the lines of the established proprieties, however deeply he may sympathize with the principal's impulse to slay the adversary out of hand. In the period with which we are dealing there is no room for doubt that the statesmen chiefly concerned with Anglo-American relations regarded one another with sincere respect, and were earnest in their desire for harmony between the peoples. They were all aware, at the same time, of deep feelings and powerful interests on both sides of the Atlantic that worked incessantly in the opposite direction. In 1818, in the midst of the negotiations for the convention of that year, a disconcerting illustration of this fact was brought before the public by the proceedings of the American general Andrew Jackson on the Spanish soil of Florida.

In the United States the most particular abode of hostility to all things British was the valley of the Mississippi—the frontier region where population was sparse but now rapidly growing. Of the causes which nourished this hostility, the most active was probably the traditional relations between the British and the Indians in both the Northwest and the Southwest. Practically every village and settlement between the mountains and the Mississippi contained inhabitants who had suffered personally from the ghastly incidents of savage warfare. That the Indians who butchered and burned and scalped throughout the West had been systematically inspired and sustained in their acts and methods by British authorities, was an ingrained conviction among the American people. The open alliance of the army in Canada with Tecumseh during the late war confirmed this conviction for generations. Long after the war, Indian bands from the remoter regions of the

Northwest made annual pilgrimages to Malden, the Canadian garrison town across the river from Detroit, and there received the long-customary gifts from the commander. The American authorities in Michigan viewed this proceeding with much anxiety and protested to Washington against its continuance. It was firmly believed by many in the United States, including so hard-headed a personage as John Quincy Adams, that the continued distribution of gifts to the Indians was deliberately calculated to insure the support of the savages in future hostilities.

In the southern part of the United States the Creek Indians, during the war with Great Britain, had, more or less under the inspiration of Tecumseh, opened war of the usual kind on the whites. The ruthless energy of Andrew Jackson soon crushed the savages, many of whom sought safety across the boundary in Florida, where Spanish authority held feeble sway. So feeble was this sway that a British force had ventured to occupy Pensacola, the capital of the province, as a base of operations against the Americans. Jackson pursued his Indian foes into Florida, and did not abandon Spanish territory till he had captured Pensacola and driven the British force out of the neighborhood.  The utter inability of Spain to maintain a semblance of effective sovereignty in Florida was made perfectly clear by these events.  After the peace of Ghent her weakness continued to be manifested in the threatening activities of hostile Indians, runaway slaves, and many varieties of outlaws along the American frontier.  The Spanish governor, in reply to complaints, acknowledged that he could not keep these people in order.  In 1817 Seminole Indians attacked United States troops on the border and Jackson, with the prestige of success in the defence of New Orleans about him, was sent to take charge of the situation. His procedure was characteristic.  He marched straight into Florida, scattering the Indians as he advanced, and seized the Spanish town of Saint Mark's.  Among the captives taken here was a substantial trader named Arbuthnot, a British subject, whose home was the island of Nassau.  He was well known to the American commander as a man of influence with the Indians, and as one who believed that the Seminoles had been unjustly treated by the United States.  Garrisoning Saint Mark's, Jackson set out for the chief town of the Seminoles, a hundred miles away, but on reaching it after a difficult march, found it deserted, and thus was unable to deliver the crushing blow that he had planned. From a white man whom he captured he discovered that a letter from Arbuthnot had warned the Indians of the impending danger and prompted their escape. Robert Ambrister, an employee of Arbuthnot and also a British subject, was captured in the vicinity of the Indian town. All the circumstances seemed to Jackson to call for summary proceedings. Returning to Saint Mark's, he brought the luckless Britons before a court martial, convicted them of various offences under the laws of war, and had Arbuthnot hanged and Ambrister shot.

The doughty general's vigor did not end with these achievements. A little later he felt obliged to go and capture Pensacola again, and teach the Spanish governor the error of his ways. This incident was not necessary, however, to set the wheels of international controversy in motion; they were spinning at top speed already. The summary execution of two British subjects by an American general at a place where the right of the victims to be secure was more apparent than the right of the commander to be at all, caused a great explosion of wrath in

England. At the very first reports of what had occurred, the press flamed with demands for the vindication of Britain's outraged honor. The cabinet were much embarrassed to refrain from serious action before the arrival of full and official information as to the affair. War might have been brought about, Castlereagh later told Rush, "if the ministry had but held up a finger." When all the facts were known, however, the government was fully justified in its caution; for on the evidence submitted it was obliged to admit that Arbuthnot and Ambrister had by their relations with the Indians forfeited the right to protection by the British Government against the military power of the United States. Jackson's high-handed proceedings in Florida were in the long run more violently assailed in his own country than abroad. The Monroe administration only with much difficulty agreed upon sustaining him, and rival politicians in Congress attacked him without mercy. Popular feeling, however, especially in the West, was enthusiastically in his favor, and eventually made him President of the United States. Not least among the influences that worked to bring him this distinction was the wide-spread tradition that in executing Arbuthnot and Ambrister he had deliberately flouted and defied Great Britain.

The correct and friendly attitude of the British Government was manifested in other incidents during this period. Even on so stubbornly contested a point as the right of search Rush had reason to believe that an agreement would have been reached if Castlereagh had been able to remain in personal supervision of the negotiations. The foreign secretary was called away to the Continent at a critical stage of the discussion, after having given very clear indications of his individual disposition to go far in yielding. In the negotiation of the treaty of commerce, also, Frederick John Robinson, the chief British representative, intimated a feeling that the American demands were too early in time rather than too objectionable in substance to be conceded.

It was inherent in the general condition of world politics that America should be seeking new things and Great Britain should be standing by the old. Especially was this the case in regard to commerce and navigation. The newcomer among maritime powers found herself barred in every direction from profitable trade by the existing system under which every

nation protected its own merchants and shipping interests by excluding foreigners from its
jurisdiction save under heavy burdens.  To the
Americans it seemed something like a violation
of natural justice that they should be forbidden
to sell a cargo of goods in Halifax or Jamaica;
yet such was British law.  It was hard to question the right of a government to exclude foreigners from its ports; but the desperate eagerness of the Americans for certain kinds of trade
led them at times to take the ground that freedom of commercial intercourse was so profoundly an interest of all mankind as fairly to
be within the domain of natural law.  Such a
trend of argument could, of course, have no
practical effect in any concrete case; the British, entrenched in commanding commercial sites
all over the globe, could and did merely
inquire what the Americans could offer for the
privileges they sought.  Bargaining of the kind
thus suggested was a very unsatisfactory process where there was such disparity between
the two parties in actual possessions.  It was
like the freedom of contract in a later day that
was alleged to be a sufficient principle on which
to base the relations of wage-earner and wage-
payer.

In the treaty of commerce and navigation of 1815, which was, as stated above, a recurrence to ante-bellum conditions, there was one provision that proved to be influential in breaking down the ancient system of commercial restriction. For the first time on record, two nations agreed by treaty to abandon the recourse to discriminating duties, Great Britain limiting her concession to her European territories. Commodities produced in these territories and the United States respectively were to pay as favorable customs duties as were paid by the products of any other nation, and tonnage duties were to be precisely the same on British and American ships in the ports of both powers. As discrimination in duties was a favorite means of carrying out the old restrictive policy, this reciprocal concession of equality was a distinct step toward a different system. It became, in fact, a model for a long line of later conventions by which the nations advanced in the path of commercial freedom. The treaty of 1815 was tentative only, being limited by its terms to four years. It was renewed for ten years by the treaty of 1818, and later was renewed indefinitely.

It is not to be gainsaid that the motive of

the powers in promoting as they did the cause
of freedom of commerce was mainly a shrewd
calculation of immediate self-interest rather
than any devotion to an abstract ideal. Equally
beyond question is it that the ideals that pervaded the intellectual atmosphere of the day
were wholly adverse to the old system. After
the Napoleonic storm had subsided, doctrines
that had played a large part in producing the
French Revolution, but had been driven to
cover by the course taken by that convulsion,
began to assume prominence in England. The
economic theories of Adam Smith and the legal
and political dogmas of Jeremy Bentham won
adherents if not yet respectability. These systems, in all their implications, were hostile to
the existing institutions of Great Britain. Underlying both philosophies was the conception of man as a free and intelligent being,
working out, each individual for himself, the
mode and content of his welfare. British commerce and industry were based upon a complex
of regulations and restrictions designed to favor
particular kinds of business and special classes
of people; and the government which distributed the favor was itself controlled by a
particular business and a special class of people.

Between the two political parties, Tory and Whig, the only important difference was as to what interests and classes should be preferred; neither contemplated a political or economic system in which preference should have no place. This latter idea found expression, however, through the radical reformers who began about 1820 to exert a perceptible influence on British thought. Between that date and 1850 a far-reaching transformation was effected in economic and political conditions, chiefly by the Whigs. Much as this party detested the Radicals, the general character of the reforms that it effected followed the lines laid out by the acute reasoning of the Benthamite school— the two Mills, Ricardo, Grote, Joseph Hume, Austin, and Molesworth.

In America the conditions which the British approached as far-distant ideals were conspicuous facts. Within the vast region controlled by the United States commercial and industrial freedom was complete. No legal barriers restricted a man's choice among the opportunities for self-betterment that beckoned in every direction. Whether he devoted his energies to farming or to manufacturing or to trade was determined solely by his judgment as to the profit to be expected; and what he should raise on his farm, what he should make in his workshop, or to whom he should sell the products of his labor, was a question to be settled by no different criterion. Politically, the freedom of the individual was only less complete. Property qualifications for the suffrage and for holding office generally prevailed, but were of consequence only in the eastern States. In the growing West, where differences of wealth were as slight and rare as all other marks of social inequality, distinctions in political rights were from the outset unknown in fact and were early banished from the law.

Thus it was true that despite the enormous differences between the two great societies of English-speaking people, a subtle force was operating to bring them together. Every step in Great Britain toward breaking down the ancient system of privilege and restriction was an approach, however unintended, toward the democratic ideal. Every step in the United States toward national consolidation involved such development and fostering of special interests, however reluctantly, as to limit perceptibly the *laissez-faire* individualism of the democratic fact. The progress of the two nations in the indicated directions was made very manifest in the history of their internal development during the decades of the thirties and the forties.

# CHAPTER II

## WHIG REFORM AND JACKSONIAN DEMOCRACY

THE transition to the full tide of Whiggery in Great Britain and of Jacksonianism in the United States was marked by the ascendancy respectively of George Canning and John Quincy Adams. Canning succeeded Castlereagh as foreign secretary in 1822, became prime minister in 1827, and after a few months died in that office. Adams was secretary of state under Monroe for eight years, 1817–25, and was President from 1825 to 1829. So largely was the interest of both these statesmen centred on foreign affairs that something distinctive in the relations of the two powers could reasonably be expected at this time. Nothing novel occurred, however, in connection with the familiar subjects of debate: the right of search, commerce, navigation, fisheries—all remained substantially as before. Yet the distinctive something did not fail to appear. In 1823 the group of policies famous collectively and individually as the Monroe Doctrine was promulgated in the President's annual message, and the fact and form and time of the announcement reflected in no small measure the influence of both Canning and Adams.

Canning did not like the American democracy. The attitude of the Foreign Office after he took charge was significantly different from what it had been under Castlereagh. If the latter in his soul felt a Tory contempt for the Americans, he took pains to keep it from affecting his diplomatic intercourse with them. Canning was not so successful in this. The truth seems to be that Castlereagh regarded his policy in European affairs as requiring that America be kept quiet and contented, so as not to interfere with the progress of really important matters. To him the great American Republic gave no concern; to Canning it was the object of distrust and fear. Yet Canning did not hesitate to make the United States an instrument of his own policy. When engaged in the operations through which, as he eloquently boasted, he "called the New World into existence to redress the balance of the Old," he sought the co-operation of the American Government. President Monroe's message of 1823 signified to a certain extent the success of Canning's advances. Its pronouncements as a whole, however, were widely at variance with the British secretary's desires and expectations, and caused him annoyance and vexation that he ultimately took no pains to conceal. He was confirmed in his feeling of dislike and distrust of the Americans and in his foreboding of danger from their rivalry with British interests in the future.

The European situation that produced the Monroe Doctrine is familiar history. A revolution in Spain that jeoparded the throne and life of the King brought military intervention by France, supported by Russia, Prussia, and Austria. The Spanish monarch was restored to his authority at home, but found himself wholly unable to regain control of his continental colonies in America, which had declared and were successfully maintaining their independence. Accordingly, he applied to the powers that had assisted him for like assistance on the other side of the Atlantic. The British Government had refused to join the other powers in the intervention in Spain, and had viewed with great uneasiness the proceedings of the French army. Tories were unpleasantly reminded by the situation of the days when Napoleonic France had possession of Spain; Whigs and the liberalizing element of the Tories were disgusted with Bourbon absolutism wherever it appeared. British commerce with the insurgent Spanish colonies was much harassed by the irregular privateering and ineffective blockades through which the Spaniards maintained the semblance, with but little of the substance, of war. This commerce had attained large proportions and all its advantages would be lost if Spanish authority should be restored; for Spain, like Britain herself, regarded colonial trade as an exclusive privilege of the mother country.

Under all the circumstances Canning was readily able, at the first manifestation of a project for intervention in behalf of Spain in America, to gain substantial support for his purpose to thwart it. An indication of interest in the general subject by Rush, the minister at London, was promptly made by Canning the occasion of a suggestion for a joint, or at least a simultaneous, declaration by the United States and Great Britain of their hostility to the threatened intervention. The idea was received with the liveliest interest at Washington and was the subject of the most serious consideration by the President, the cabinet, and even Jefferson and Madison, whose opinions were confidentially sought by Monroe. Abundant reasons were perceived for refraining from formal association with Great Britain in a declaration of policy, but the wisdom of some pronouncement was not questioned by any. Accordingly, the familiar paragraphs were inserted in the President's annual message to Congress in December. After a general expression of sympathy with the peoples of Europe in their struggles for liberty and happiness, and of a purpose, nevertheless, to abstain from taking part in any wars there, the momentous declaration was made:

With the movements in this hemisphere we are, of necessity, more immediately connected, and by causes which must be obvious to all enlightened and impartial observers. The political system of the allied powers is essentially different in this respect from that of America. The difference proceeds from that which exists in their respective governments. And to the defence of our own, which has been achieved by the loss of so much blood and treasure, and matured by the wisdom of their most enlightened citizens, and under which we have enjoyed such unexampled felicity, this whole nation is devoted. We owe it, therefore, to candor, and to the amicable relations existing between the United States and those powers, to declare that we should consider any attempt on their part to extend their system to any portion of this hemisphere as dangerous to our peace and safety. With the existing colonies or dependencies of any European power we have not interfered and shall not interfere. But with the governments who have declared their independence and maintained it, and whose independence we have, on great consideration and on just principles, acknowledged, we could not view any interposition for the purpose of oppressing them, or controlling in any other manner their destiny, by any European power, in any other light than as the manifestation of an unfriendly disposition toward the United States. . . .

. . . It is impossible that the allied powers should extend their political system to any portion of either continent without endangering our peace and happiness; nor can any one believe that our southern brethren, if left to themselves, would adopt it of their own accord. It is equally impossible, therefore, that we should behold such interposition, in any form, with indifference.

So far as concerned the particular subject that evoked these paragraphs, they were entirely efficacious. No possibility was left of intervention in America by the allied powers. As a matter of fact the project was dead before the President spoke; for Canning had secured assurances from the French Government that it would not take part in the proposed action, and without French aid the powers would be as helpless as the Spanish King himself. This situation was not known outside of diplomatic circles when Monroe's message appeared. In consequence, the public announcement, in such

uncompromising terms, of the attitude of the
United States appeared very decisive and made
a prodigious sensation both at home and abroad.
That so weighty a judgment on a question of
world politics should emanate from Washington,
satisfied the spirit of the most ardent patriots
in America; in England the Whigs and Radicals
rejoiced at the alliance of the two English-speaking nations for the defence of liberty against
the despots of the Holy Alliance, and even the
Tories found something to approve in the aid
given by the Americans to a keen stroke of
British policy.  The press on both sides of the
Atlantic teemed for a time with expressions of
amicable feeling.

Canning accepted with complacency the flattering tributes to his skill and astuteness in
bringing America to the aid of Britain.  He
had, however, no illusions about the realities of
the case.  He perceived at first sight, in the
salving ointment of Monroe's message, a very
unpleasant and dangerous insect.  In the paragraphs that have been quoted there was, he
saw, a conspicuous lack of care to discriminate
precisely among the "European powers," so as
to exclude Great Britain from the warning
addressed to them.  It was not hard to read

the document as embodying the claim that the American continents were to be reserved for republican, as contrasted with monarchic, institutions — a reservation that would shut out George IV of Great Britain as effectively as it would Ferdinand VII of Spain. In another part of the message, moreover, quite unrelated to that which dealt with the matter of the European intervention on behalf of Spain, a pronouncement was made that revealed with distinctness the spirit suspected by Canning. Apropos of negotiations with Russia concerning the respective claims to the Pacific coast, this passage occurred:

. . . the occasion has been judged proper for asserting as a principle in which the rights and interests of the United States are involved, that the American continents, by the free and independent condition which they have assumed and maintain, are henceforth not to be considered as subjects for future colonization by any European powers.

Here again was a warning to all European powers, and in connection with a matter—colonization—that was a specialty of Great Britain. Canning was assured that the reference in the passage was to a reported project of Russia for a southward extension of her settlements on

the Pacific coast of America. He took pains
to declare, however, that his government did
not accept the principle laid down, and he
emphasized his protest by withdrawing from
association with the United States in the negotiations at Saint Petersburg by which the limit
of Russian claims in America was fixed.

Canning was right in restraining his enthusiasm over Monroe's message. It was, in fact,
the pronunciamento of a great democracy just
arrived at aggressive self-consciousness. Its underlying spirit was in very truth antagonism,
so far as concerned affairs of the Western Hemisphere, to all monarchic Europe, Great Britain
included. The significant passages in the document owed their phraseology, in great part,
to John Quincy Adams; and he has left on record abundant evidence that no sentiment of
attachment to Great Britain would ever influence him to except her from the sweep of
a policy devised to promote the interest and
glory of his own government. Canning instinctively resented the spirit of which Adams
was the particular embodiment. Hence the
marked subsidence, after 1823, of the demonstrative warmth which the Monroe Doctrine
of that year temporarily produced between the

two governments. They had become serious rivals for the controlling interest in American affairs.

During the last two years of Canning's life, 1825–27, the diplomatic situation in general was very unpleasant. What he had tried most diligently to prevent, when he summoned the New World to solve the problems of the Old, seemed near to realization, namely, the confronting of monarchic Europe by a solidly republican America. The establishment of monarchy in Brazil he had regarded with much satisfaction, and Iturbide's imperial enterprise in Mexico seemed to him likely to provide a useful counterpoise to the influence of the United States. The melancholy failure of Iturbide confirmed the disappointment that Monroe's message created. It only remained to oppose at every point the ambition of the United States, and to be unceasingly watchful against the development of her claims. In a familiar letter to Bagot, now ambassador at Saint Petersburg, of July 29, 1824, Canning urged haste in concluding with Russia a convention assuring to Great Britain the right of navigation in Behring Sea and Straits. "There is very nice 'bobbing for whale' they tell me, *ipsis Behringi in faucibus,* which must be guarded." And then he added, with a prophetic vision that the future was remarkably to verify: "We shall have a squabble with the Yankees yet in and about these regions."

The most explicit revelation of Canning's feelings and policy at this time is seen in a secret despatch to Vaughan, the British minister at Washington, recently brought to light by Professor E. D. Adams. It is dated February 8, 1826, and relates to certain discussions concerning Cuba.

The general maxim that our interest and those of the United States are essentially the same, etc., etc., is one that cannot be too readily admitted, when put forward by the United States.

But we must not be the dupes of this conventional language of courtesy.

The avowed pretension of the United States to put themselves at the head of the confederacy of all the Americas, and to sway that confederacy against Europe, (Great Britain included), is *not* a pretension identified with our interests, or one that we can countenance as tolerable.

It is however a pretension which there is no use in contesting in the abstract; but we must not say anything that seems to admit the principle.[1]

When this note was penned, the two governments were in the midst of a long and

[1] Proceedings of the Massachusetts Historical Society, November, 1912, p. 234.

disagreeable controversy over the trade with
the British-American colonies.  Parliament, engaged in revising the Navigation Laws, opened
the colonial ports in America to foreign vessels
on certain conditions in 1825.  The United
States refused to accept the conditions, and
took ground, both through the Department of
State and in Congress, that seemed to question
the right of Great Britain to impose restrictions
at her discretion on commerce in her own colonies.  To Canning and his party this was but
another exhibition of the "forwardness, not to
say impudence," that was typical of the American policy, especially when directed by Adams.
It was met therefore by an open and unmistakable snub.  An Order in Council closed the
West Indian ports absolutely to American ships.
The order was issued while Gallatin was on his
way to England, for the special purpose of settling by negotiation this and other questions
between the two governments.  On his arrival
he was met by a flat refusal to discuss in
any way the matter of the West Indian trade,
and was left entirely in the dark as to the
reason for the unexpected attitude of the government.

Gallatin's despatches after his arrival, in

August, 1826, indicate very well the impression made by the Canning administration.

There is certainly an alteration in the disposition of this government since the year 1818, when I was here before. Lord Castlereagh and Mr. Robinson had it more at heart to cherish friendly relations than Mr. Canning and Mr. Huskisson. The difference may, however, be in the times rather than in the men. Treated in general with considerable arrogance till the last war, with great attention, if not respect, during the years that followed it, the United States are now an object of jealousy; and a policy founded on that feeling has been avowed.

This was written to Clay. To Adams Gallatin wrote:

. . . it is impossible for me not to see and feel the temper that prevails here toward us . . . quite changed from what it was in 1815–1821; nearly as bad as before the last war, only they hate more and despise less, though they still affect to conceal hatred under the appearance of contempt.

This diplomatic irritation did not penetrate deeply into the national tissues. Its cause lay largely in the personalities of Canning and Adams. Party politics on both sides of the ocean contributed somewhat to increase and prolong the inflammation. But Canning died in August, 1827; and it is probably more than a mere coincidence that in that month and the

following no less than three conventions were
signed for the provisional settlement of questions at issue between the two governments.
By these conventions the joint occupation of
Oregon and the commercial treaty of 1815 were
renewed indefinitely, subject to abrogation by
either party on twelve months' notice, and the
northeastern boundary was referred to arbitration. The West India trade situation was thus
left the sole disturbing feature of the relations between the governments. It played a
part in the presidential campaign of 1828, in
which Adams failed of re-election. The succeeding administration, that of General Jackson,
with Martin Van Buren as secretary of state,
promptly reversed the policy of the United
States, dropped the contentions that Adams had
sustained, and came to an agreement with Great
Britain on her own terms. In the autumn of
1830 commerce between the United States and
the British West Indies, with some limitations
still remaining, was reopened, and the controversy over the subject ceased to trouble the
intercourse of the governments.

Pending the final disposition of this question
the long domination of the Tory party in Great
Britain came to an end. Incompatibilities of.

personality and principles between Canning and his friends on one side and the ultra-Tory element led by the Duke of Wellington on the other, hastened this event. In 1830 the Whigs, headed by Earl Grey, assumed the reins of power and entered upon a famous era of internal reform. Domestic politics on both sides of the Atlantic assumed an absorbing importance, and the diplomatic relations became cordially calm.

The far-reaching transformation, industrial, social, and political, that marked the decade of the thirties in the United Kingdom had its culmination rather than its inception under the régime of the Whigs. The forces making for change became very manifest immediately upon the restoration of peace in 1815. A sudden shift from the condition of general European war to that of universal peace was necessarily accompanied by a vast displacement and readjustment in the field of trade and industry. British commerce and manufactures had flourished greatly during the war, thanks to the immunity of the United Kingdom from the ravages of contending armies, and to her unquestioned control of the sea. With peace the peoples of the Continent resumed their normal productive activities and British trade heavily declined. Prices fell; complications in the currency, due to the suspension of specie payments, aggravated the troubles; bad harvests recurred at unfortunate intervals; and the great change in progress in the methods of manufacturing, owing to the introduction of machinery, contributed in its turn a quota of evil. The general result was unsettlement, discontent, and from time to time severe distress among the working classes, both agricultural and industrial. Into the field thus well prepared came agitators of the political type, Radicals, preaching the doctrines of the French and Americans, and demanding universal suffrage, voting by ballot, and other reforms of a sort to shock the Tories beyond expression.

To the governing classes these popular movements were but a manifestation of the subversive spirit that had animated the French Revolution and was still troubling the Continental rulers. In 1819, after a fatal conflict between the people and the military at Manchester, Parliament enacted the "Six Acts," which imposed severe restrictions on the press and on the holding of public meetings. These were the methods of suppressing political opposition

that were in use on the Continent, and they
were felt by the less reactionary element in
Great Britain to be inconsistent with the traditions of English liberty. Whether because of
the odium thus incurred, or because of their very
effectiveness itself, the Six Acts marked practically the culmination of the policy of aggressive severity against the Radical agitation.
It became increasingly clear to Whigs and liberal Tories alike that the recurring popular disturbances were due quite as much to deeply-
lying economic causes as to the mere idealism
and ambition of visionaries and Radicals. The
advent of Canning to the position of chief influence in the government in 1822 contributed
to the change in the trend of official feeling.
Under Castlereagh's dominance the cordiality
between Great Britain and the allied monarchs
of the Continent in foreign policy promoted a
correspondence in domestic policy. Canning's
spectacular and defiant break with the powers,
and his open support of insurgents in Europe
and in America, gave inspiration and hope to
those who were looking for extensive, if not
technically Radical, changes in ancient British
institutions.

The anticipated process of reform promptly

made its appearance. Huskisson, brought by Canning to the presidency of the Board of Trade, was deeply imbued with the doctrines of Adam Smith as to keeping the hands of the government off commerce and industry. The ancient restrictions through which business was parcelled out among particular groups and secured to them at all hazards, were incompatible with Huskisson's principles and were, moreover, at present working to the disadvantage of the favored classes and producing the disturbances that were so significant signs of the times. First, the shipping industry received Huskisson's attention. The Navigation Laws had for a century and a half given monopolistic protection to British merchant-vessels and had secured for them a clear control of the carrying trade of the world. The United States was now contesting that control and was using in the competition the same methods by which Great Britain had secured it, namely, a monopolistic protection of American shipping against all foreign rivals. Parliament dropped in 1823 the rigidity of the old policy by authorizing the government to suspend the application of the laws through agreements with other governments for reciprocal advantages. This was the beginning of the end of the old system. A quarter of a century elapsed before the final step was taken that opened the ports of Great Britain without restriction to the shipping of all the world.

In the next two years laws were passed giving recognition to the new conditions in manufacturing that the industrial revolution had brought into prominence. Labor troubles in the modern sense, contests over wages between factory-owners and employees, had become a conspicuous element in the popular agitations of the time. Under the ancient legal system the employers had every advantage in the chronic struggle. Great as was the fear in Parliament of the working classes, it gave way before clear evidence that the law imposed upon them something near to the lot of the slave. To help himself was a right that the spirit of the day regarded as inherent in every British freeman. Hence the old statutes were repealed which prohibited meetings and associations of workmen for getting increase of wages, and even forbade artisans absolutely to leave the country.

The progress of this reforming legislation was followed with deep concern and covert hos-

tility by the extreme Tories. It did not so
directly affect the ruling aristocracy as a whole,
however, as to excite a decisive opposition.
Quite otherwise was the case with the Corn
Law, on which the rents of the landowners
were believed absolutely to depend. Protection to the domestic grain-growers was by this
legislation ingeniously complete. Duties on imported grain varied with the price in England;
importation was prohibited so long as the price
was under a maximum figure; and exportation
was stimulated by bounties when the price fell
below a minimum figure. Despite the guarantee thus apparently established that Great
Britain should produce the food for her own
people at a fair and steady cost, there was
continual friction over the matter. Prices
fluctuated disastrously with variations of the
weather, and were never low enough for the
consumers or high enough for the farmers and
the landlords. Parliament was called upon
repeatedly to consider exceptional modifications of the system, in order to check distress
among the farmers or the working classes. Demands became frequent and loud for a radical
change that should do away with the high protection to grain-growers; but here the aristo-

cratic landed interest by which both parties were controlled stood firm and unyielding. The Corn Law was to prove the last stronghold of the old system to be carried by the rising middle-class industrial interest. After the death of Canning in 1827 his powerful patronage was seen to have been indispensable to the reforming projects of Huskisson; for there soon came open rupture between the Canningites and the ultra-Tories headed by the Duke of Wellington. Differences about the Corn Law had much to do with this dissension, though two other subjects took precedence in practical consideration when the reforming influence got the upper hand.

The first of these subjects was Catholic emancipation. In 1829 the general disqualification of Catholics for holding office or sitting in Parliament was finally removed. This action had long been sought by enlightened statesmen, and had failed of realization in law only through the dogged resistance of royalty itself. The relief act of 1829 was significant less from its content than from the means through which its passage, despite the sullen opposition of the King and a few bigoted advisers, was made unavoidable. Daniel O'Connell, between 1823 and 1829, made Catholic Ireland self-conscious and strong enough to paralyze entirely the authority of the legal government. He did this without bloodshed and without giving a chance to his adversaries to use against him with any success the processes of the ordinary law or to find ground for resort to exceptional measures. His method was agitation, of a species so astutely controlled and regulated as to make the maximum impression with the minimum opportunity for lawlessness. The feature of his triumph that caused the deepest alarm in the ruling class was the severance of the Irish tenantry from almost slavish dependence on their landlords. The creation thus of an independent spirit in the mass of the Irish population was destined to produce most revolutionary results in the long run on the relations between England and Ireland; its immediate influence on the political movements in Great Britain was of the utmost concern to the class that was opposing the onward sweep of reform.

The removal of disabilities from the Catholics was effected while the Tory cabinet of Wellington and Peel was still in power. A year later, in 1830, the Whigs, led by Earl Grey and Brougham, came into control for the first time in a quarter of a century, and at once opened the famous struggle for Parliamentary reform. The demand for this reform received a great impulse from the revolutionary wave that swept over the Continent, and the popular agitation in Great Britain, reflecting the methods of O'Connell's late operations in Ireland, assumed a very threatening aspect. The Tories fought with dogged energy to retain the ancient power and privilege of the landed interest. Two years of violent political strife resulted, however, in the enactment of the reform. Through its provisions the House of Commons ceased to be under the control of the landed aristocracy and became fairly representative of the industrial class that was assuming such importance in the growing towns. The apportionment of seats among the constituencies was based in some measure upon the number of the population, thus recognizing a principle that was dear to the democratic reformer. Moreover, while the landed aristocracy still retained its control of the House of Lords, the passage of the Reform Bill had finally been effected by a proceeding that showed how, in a contest between the two houses, the Commons could constitutionally carry the day.

The Parliamentary reform of 1832 did not make Great Britain a democracy, but it put in a very clear light a trend of social and political progress that must narrow the distance between the British and the American systems. All the reforming movements that have been noticed promoted liberty, in the sense of removing from some class of the population restrictions which, however valuable at one time, had lost their utility. In the United States the restrictions had never existed, because they had never been useful; and for that reason and in the sense suggested America had led Great Britain in respect to liberty. The era of the Reform Act was signalized by the appearance of political practices that were new and terrifying in England. Associations for partisan agitation among the townspeople were larger, wealthier, and better organized than had ever been the case before. Both leaders and followers in these political unions displayed a high degree of genuine skill in the game of politics and beat the aristocracy in the field where it claimed to be alone qualified to appear. The repressive legislation of 1819 was no longer in effect, so far as its most rigorous features were concerned, and the British people enjoyed in

far larger measure than any other European
nation the liberty to organize and assemble
for peaceful discussion and to express opinions
in speech or print. Popular sentiment was
readily articulate. Doctrines much too radical for the possibility of adoption were nevertheless freely canvassed. The periodical press
was expanded and cheapened to correspond to
the widening of political interest and intelligence. In all these conditions there was a
fundamental bond of sympathy between Great
Britain and the United States. The progressive Radicals in England were conscious of this,
and systematically adduced American examples
in support of their demands for reforms. Across
the Atlantic the Americans, so far as they were
informed of British conditions, threw their sympathy with the Radicals. The Whig species
of reform aroused but a qualified enthusiasm
in the United States. It was Whig reform, however, that was alone destined to be practically
feasible in Great Britain for many decades to
come.

After 1832 the reformed Parliament, under
Whig control, continued the process of removing inveterate abuses. With many of its greatest measures, such as Poor-Law reform and the

rationalizing of municipal government, our concern is too slight for more than passing mention. Other legislation, however, had a definite bearing on relations with the United States. In 1833 an act was passed abolishing slavery in the British West Indies, by a process that became actually complete five years later. In 1835 the ancient methods of impressment in recruiting for the navy were practically ended by legislation regulating the procedure and at the same time encouraging voluntary enlistment by bounties and pensions.

The abolition of slavery in the West Indian colonies marked the triumph of a long agitation, begun by Wilberforce and continued by the Quakers and Buxton. The African slave-trade had been prohibited by Parliament, largely through Wilberforce's efforts, as early as 1807, only a year before a like prohibition was enacted by the Congress of the United States. British and American vessels were thus excluded from a very lucrative business, but the humanitarian purpose of the legislation was not in any large measure achieved, for the trade continued to flourish. Under the continuous pressure of the Abolitionists the British Government sought to arrange by treaty for the co-operation of other governments in suppressing the traffic. The subject was repeatedly brought up in conference with the representatives of the United States, and a treaty was actually agreed to in 1824, but failed through the unwillingness of Great Britain to accept amendments made by the Senate. The difference between the two governments over the right of visitation and search was the real cause of the failure. It was clear that the slave-trade could never be extinguished save by some arrangement for an international patrol of the coasts and seas where the traffic was carried on. Such arrangement would necessarily involve the examination by a war-ship of suspected vessels flying colors other than those of the overhauling cruiser. A reciprocal authorization of such procedure as between American and British cruisers the United States would never consent to; since it was held to admit the right of a British captain to search a ship bearing the American flag, and this the United States was firm in its resolution never to concede. The British were equally tenacious in opposing any kind of arrangement that might be construed as an abandonment of the right.

The long-standing tension over the right of

search thus prevented the two great English-speaking peoples from uniting for the effective suppression of a business that was admitted by both to be a scandal to civilization. Nor was the situation improved when Parliament enacted the laws that practically put an end to impressment, of which the right of search was an incident. Nothing in this legislation formally abolished the old system of recruiting, and the Foreign Office remained as tenacious of the claim to take British sailors from foreign ships as Parliament was of the undoubted right to take them by force wherever the royal jurisdiction extended. Whatever the era of reform effected in respect to the practice, the time had not yet come when the theory of personal liberty for Britons would extend to that class on whose service the safety of the empire was believed to be in a special way dependent.

Conditions in the United States also contributed to prevent the harmony of the governments in respect to the slave-trade. The slaveholding interest, concentrated in the cotton-growing States, became a powerful factor in politics during the twenties and thirties. Though there was no important sentiment in favor of the African slave-trade, there was always a base and lawless element in the Southern population who were ready to take part in the illicit operations through which small numbers of negroes were often introduced.  In 1820 a violent political contest arose in Congress over an issue of internal policy respecting slavery, and thenceforth the Southern politicians were very sensitive to any movements affecting the institution. Abolitionism of a vehement type made its appearance in the North in the early thirties, almost simultaneously with a barbarous insurrection of slaves in Virginia.  The two events combined to cause deep alarm in the South, and the feeling made the discussion of any phase of the slavery question highly inexpedient to politicians.  Then came the emancipation of the slaves of the British West Indies.  This action, hailed with joy by the Abolitionists, confirmed the uneasiness in the Southern States of the Union.  Resentment toward the British was increased by a series of cases in which the colonial authorities of the Bahamas and the Bermudas forcibly liberated the slaves who happened to be on American coasting vessels that came within British jurisdiction through stress of weather, wreck, and mutiny.  That the feeling aroused by these various occurrences had an influence in making futile the efforts to agree concerning the slave-trade cannot be doubted; yet the difference as to the right of search on the high seas was the vital cause of failure.

The growth and self-consciousness of the slaveholding interest in the United States had a close relation to other phases of the development of the American democracy. I have said above that in the Jacksonian era there was a narrowing of the interval which separated the American from the British ideals of social structure and policy. In Great Britain the trend was steadily, as has been noted, toward removal of the restrictions that sustained established interests and privileges. In the United States, on the other hand, a pronounced movement appeared toward the creation of similar restrictions. The powers of the general government had already been devoted, through diplomacy and legislation, to vigorous efforts for the protection and promotion of foreign trade and the mercantile marine. During the twenties a systematic agitation was begun for a like degree of governmental activity in behalf of the nascent-manufactures of the Union. Henry Clay, a statesman of extraordinary popularity, led this

movement on its political side, and sustained it
by fervent appeals for an "American system"
that should make the United States in all respects economically self-sufficient, and independent of foreign, especially British, producers.
The result was tariff legislation, culminating
in 1828, by which heavy protective duties were
imposed on textiles, iron, and other leading commodities.

Protectionism of this species was not destined,
however, to be permanent. Accepted with much
misgiving in the North and West, it aroused
violent hostility in the slaveholding States of
the South. Their sole commercial product was
cotton, and three-fourths of the crop was exported, mostly to Great Britain. To them,
therefore, the high tariff meant only a disastrous increase of taxation, for the benefit of
the manufacturers of the North. A bitter opposition to the new system was carried on by
the State of South Carolina, involving serious
threats of a dissolution of the Union. The
policy that was proclaimed as necessary to the
free life and full development of the republic
thus proved fraught with peril to its very existence. Clay himself bowed before the storm
that he had evoked, and took the lead in legis-

lation through which, by stages beginning in 1833, the tariff was so reduced that the protective features entirely disappeared. The slaveholders whose system exemplified the extreme of curtailment of personal liberty thus proved the successful champions of a policy that insured the fullest freedom in respect to property.

The failure of protectionism was a feature of the era of Andrew Jackson. It is with good reason that this President's name has become descriptive of a period of American history. Jacksonian democracy designates a psychological phase in the growth of the republic. It was the phase in which a people became fully aware of its freedom, unity, and power, and began to strive, with pathetically crude and ineffective means, to make a useful application of these qualities. Jackson was the first President from west of the Appalachian Mountains. With him began the conspicuous influence of the Mississippi valley in the American Government. That vast region was by 1830 making great strides in population and prosperity. Steam transportation on its innumerable rivers and lakes gave a great stimulus to settlement and trade. The social type still remained, however, that of the frontier, slightly refined, and this was the type that Jackson exemplified and impressed upon the nation as a whole. Abounding physical vigor, courage, self-confidence, resourcefulness, fervid patriotism, Mosaic morality with a primitive interpretation, a narrow intellectual horizon—these were the characteristics that were predominant. The problems of social life in the simple conditions that generally prevailed were readily enough solved by a people of this type. Where circumstances called for the settlement of questions of some complexity, such as the growth of the nation brought to the front, the popular feeling was often that of irritability and suspicion toward those who professed to be able to furnish answers on the basis of a scientific knowledge that was beyond the reach of the average man.

This democratic distrust of the expert played a large part in the conflict between President Jackson and the United States Bank, a conflict that most clearly exhibited the tendencies of the times. The bank was chartered by Congress and had since 1816 served a useful purpose as an agency for the fiscal operations of the treasury and also for providing a currency by its note issues. Jackson formed the opinion that the bank was a dangerous institution, of a mon-

opolistic character and repugnant to the Constitution and to sound public policy.  On the
question of renewing its charter the financial
and commercial interests of the nation rallied
strongly to the support of the bank and were
sustained by a majority in Congress.  The President was able, however, after a spectacular
struggle, to defeat the renewal and to destroy
the bank.  His economic reasoning was crude
and primitive, but his appeal to the people
against the moneyed class that he said was
oppressing them struck a responsive chord,
especially in his native West.  In a campaign
that was fought chiefly on the issue of the bank
Jackson was re-elected in triumph to the presidency.  In popular estimation his patriotic service in destroying the bank took rank with that
performed when, as was commonly believed, he
saved his country from the yoke of the British
by the victory at New Orleans.

The democratic trend in the political operations of the Jacksonian era might be traced in
many phases of public life.  One only may be
referred to here.  It was in Jackson's time that
the so-called "spoils system," not unknown to
the practice of the politicians before, became
openly and on principle employed in manning

the civil service of the National Government. Many influences united, of course, in producing this result. What never failed to win support for the system, however, was the contention that it was democratic—that it was based on the idea that where equality was the order of the day there must be no permanent tenure, no monopoly, in the service of the people, but every individual must be presumed equally qualified for the service, every one must have the chance in rotation to perform the duties of office. Just as the business of banking was to be open to all without restriction, so the offices of the government must be open to all. And no safer test was available of the people's will as to the tenant of appointive office at any particular time than the result of a contest for the great elective offices. The voice of the successful party was the voice of the people, and the choice of the party leader was the sufficient index in any particular case of the party's wish as to the tenant of an office. In vain was it pointed out by the well-informed that patronage of this type was a conspicuous feature of the British governmental system and a mainstay of aristocratic ascendancy. American public opinion was incredulous or undaunted before this argument, and sustained the spoils system without flinching in the face of the evils that it increasingly involved.

The era of Jacksonism in America and Whig reform in Great Britain was marked by a significant change in the character and extent of the information about the republic that was embodied in the British literature of the day. For a decade and more after the Treaty of Ghent Tory sentiment had predominated in both travellers' books[1] and the periodical press whenever the United States was the subject of discussion. Radicals, humanitarians, agriculturists, interested in the conditions among the common people, found somewhat to commend in the bounty of nature and the material comfort and prosperity of man. Social, intellectual, and spiritual conditions generally impressed the Briton as repulsive and intolerable. Politics and government, so far as they were at all intelligible, seemed unbalanced, incoherent, and corrupt. These views of the United States were systematically and repeatedly set forth, with all the effect of skilled literary massing and polish, in the great Tory organ of the day, the *Quarterly Review*. Its distinguished Whig rival,

[1] See the valuable article by E. D. Adams, "The British Traveler in America," in *Political Science Quarterly*, June, 1914.

the *Edinburgh Review*, was less harsh in judgment on things social and political, but, because of its patronizing irony, not less offensive to the Americans.  In 1820 Sydney Smith published in the *Edinburgh Review* his famous series of questions concerning the culture of Jonathan as compared with that of John: "In the four quarters of the globe, who reads an American book? or goes to an American play? or looks at an American picture or statue? . . . Finally, under which of the old tyrannical governments of Europe is every sixth man a slave, whom his fellow creatures may buy and sell and torture?"

The *North American Review* and other publications took up the cudgels for the Americans with spirit, and a wordy warfare raged through many years.  By the judicious the controversy was deprecated; for it obviously stirred up ill feeling and misunderstandings on both sides of the ocean.  The great British reviews were regularly reprinted in the United States, and though their circulation was small and confined chiefly to the towns of the seaboard, all criticism of the Americans was diligently reproduced in the local periodicals, and the exasperation was spread to the remotest regions of the Union. In Great Britain the influence of the quarterlies was chiefly with the ruling class; but here again their ideas penetrated to the lower social strata, especially through the clergy, and confirmed the impression that the Americans were an anarchic, godless, brutal crew. In many cases the deterrent effect of such impression was welcomed by authorities of church and state whose charges sought to escape the misery of recurrent agricultural distress by emigration. Piety and patriotism both required that the emigrant should seek a home on British rather than American soil—should turn to the Canadas and avoid the United States.

After the accession of the Whigs to power, and while their reforms were in progress, British literary judgments about America began to reflect a less hostile spirit. Travellers reported more that was tolerable in the working of democratic customs and institutions, while the reviews conceded the existence of a rudimentary literature in the writings of Irving, Bryant, Cooper, Simms, and a few others. Harriet Martineau's descriptions and estimates of social and intellectual tendencies, while none too flattering, differed much in sympathy and accuracy from most that had preceded. Tocqueville's profound study, appearing in 1835 and attracting wide-spread attention at once in Great Britain, gave strong support to the revision of opinion concerning the American democracy. On the other side Mrs. Trollope's "Domestic Life of the Americans," published in 1832, with its clever and cattish caricatures, inflamed the old animosities, which a never-ending train of Tory travellers, with far less of vivacity and of malice, contributed to keep glowing. Finally, it is to be noted that in 1835 appeared the first important literary production of Richard Cobden, treating the economic forces of the United States with much analytic power and from a novel point of view. His vision of the transforming influence of American agriculture and commerce, as well as of manufactures when once the initial obstacles should be overcome, was not confused by suspicions as to the religious, moral, or political soundness of the people. He was by training one of the middle class of English society, a Manchester manufacturer, and the lack of culture that disturbed so many British observers in America did not affect Cobden's perception of the economic strength that was developing. The thesis of his essay was that Great Britain's leading position among the powers of the world was in far greater peril from the economic competition of the United States than from the diplomatic or military rivalry of any European governments. War with the Americans he regarded as impossible. In commerce and manufactures, however, he believed they were destined to take the lead, because of their enormous population and resources. His conclusion was that British policy should be directed more with reference to American conditions than along the ancient lines of the balance of power in Europe. The size of Russia's army or of France's navy should be of less interest to the government than the number of cotton looms in the United States or the statistics of her merchant marine. All restrictions that hampered the fullest development of British commerce and industry must be abolished, and the first of these to go must be that main bulwark of the aristocratic ascendancy, the Corn Law.

Thus Cobden made the United States the text of his earliest sermon against militarism and protectionism. Through the thirty years that were to follow of successful agitation and of profound influence on English policy, he never deviated from cordial appreciation and sympathy for the institutions and ideals of the

American Republic. His influence became important, however, only somewhat later than the period with which we are now dealing. The Anti-Corn-Law League took shape and position under his leadership in the late thirties, and achieved its crown of success in 1846. It is more than a coincidence that this was the year that saw the last element of protection banished from the tariff law of the United States.

That part of British public opinion concerning America which was based upon the printed accounts of travel and personal observation had no counterpart in American public opinion concerning Great Britain. Few Americans visited the United Kingdom, and of those who did so the number who published their impressions was negligible. Some opportunity to form judgments of the British individually, if not in the mass, was afforded by those who came and settled in the United States. There was in the twenties and thirties a continuous stream of immigration from all parts of the United Kingdom. The dimensions of the stream cannot be known from any trustworthy statistics. A sprinkling of English, Scots, and Irish was to be found throughout the Union. The Catholic Irish congregated clannishly in the towns and were already exciting the antagonism that was to be so serious in the middle of the century. The other elements nowhere became numerous or assertive enough to produce a perceptible impression. They were mostly artisans or farmers, Presbyterians or English dissenters, well adapted to conform without friction to the social conditions into which they came. A large proportion of them had left their homes under pressure of social or economic discontent and distress, and so far as they gave a basis for opinion as to Great Britain they confirmed the conviction that the people there were a very decent body, shamefully oppressed by a haughty group of peers and clergy. This opinion derived new support from the fate of the Chartist movement in the late thirties. The demands of the Chartists were to Americans elementary political rights; and the summary treatment of the agitation strengthened the notion that English liberty under Whig domination was as unreal as under the Tories.

# CHAPTER III

## THE ROARING FORTIES: POLK AND PALMERSTON

In 1837 Martin Van Buren succeeded Andrew Jackson as President of the United States and Victoria succeeded William IV on the throne of the United Kingdom. These changes did not signify any open reversal of governmental policy in either case. Van Buren was Jackson's own choice for the succession and was thoroughly identified with the Democratic Party that followed Jackson; the Whig cabinet of Lord Melbourne continued to direct affairs under the Queen as they had done under the King. Yet from this date the relations among the English-speaking peoples lost the tone of cordiality that had characterized them for a decade, and entered upon a protracted period of hostility and tension, approaching more than once to the verge of war.

First among the conditions that revealed the new trend of things was a political ebullition of serious proportions in Canada. In

neither of the two provinces bearing this name
had the development of political and economic
life since 1815 been calm and satisfactory.
Party strife was keen on lines that strongly
suggested the history of the United States just
before it broke away from Great Britain. The
chief organs of government in each province were
a governor appointed by the crown, a legislative
council likewise appointed, and an assembly
elected by the people. In both the Canadas the
central point of constitutional strife was the tenure and powers of the legislative council. When
in 1791 the existing province of Quebec was divided into the two provinces of Lower Canada
and Upper Canada, it was expected that the
one should be distinctively the centre of a policy
adapted to the character and feelings of the
French population, and the other the particular
home of the English. In the course of time,
however, the English element in Lower Canada
gained largely on the French through immigration. In the thirties the ratio of English to
French was possibly as high as one to three.
Compared with the conservative, easy-going
French element the newcomers were radical
and aggressive and they aroused strong misgivings
in their compatriots. Political parties tended

steadily to follow the lines of race. In the assembly the numerically stronger French easily maintained the ascendancy, but the members of the legislative council were selected by the governors chiefly from the English element. Hence a persistent demand from the assembly that the council should be made elective. On all subjects of party contest the antagonism between the two houses, with the governor sustaining the council, was intense, and the hostility was but the central point of a far-reaching race conflict.

In Upper Canada there was no difference of nationalities to fix the lines of the party conflicts. The issues here turned chiefly on the rivalries between the original settlers and the later arrivals, the latter being almost entirely British, with only a small though active element of immigrants from the United States. The Loyalists by whom, at the end of the American Revolution, the colony was practically created, became by their landed wealth, their substantial character, and their political experience, as well as by the deliberate recognition of the home government, a social and political aristocracy in the province. By the thirties a relatively narrow group of this class

had firmly in their control all branches of the
administration save the assembly. The opposition party consisted of the later immigrants,
whose origin and characteristics were much like
those of the people who were filling up the
neighboring borders of the United States. They
were of the dissenting creeds, for example, while
the aristocratic party, known commonly as the
United Empire Loyalists, preserved in general
a connection with the Church of England. This
matter of ecclesiastical attachment had no little influence in the critical politics of the time;
for profound issues of educational and fiscal
policy turned on the conflicting interests of the
various sects.

The aspect of affairs in Lower Canada assumed a threatening character in 1836. For
four years prior to that date the assembly had
refused to vote the money for the judicial and
administrative service. The British home government was much embarrassed by the situation; for the Whig traditions of the cabinet
pointed to sympathy with the ostensible principles of the popular party, and both the English
Radicals and the Irish followers of O'Connell vigorously sustained the cause of the discontented French as the cause of liberty and

democracy against aristocratic privilege. On
the other hand, the conservative element of the
Whigs stood out stiffly for the protection of the
English-speaking minority in Canada, and this
position was taken also by a special commission sent out to examine the situation. Some
concessions offered by this commission had
merely the effect, however, of evoking a fresh
manifestation of recalcitrance by the majority
in the assembly at Quebec, and the British
cabinet was forced to appeal to Parliament for
decisive action. Accordingly, a series of resolutions was passed in May, 1837, authorizing
the governor-general to pay the arrears due
for the public service without waiting for the
vote of the assembly, declaring it inexpedient
to make the legislative council elective, and
denying other important demands of the French
party.

The result of this action was insurrection.
In November, after a period of violent agitation led by the Frenchman Papineau and a
few British sympathizers, armed uprisings took
place in several French communities. There
was little organization and no discernible co-
operation in the various movements, and they
were all quickly suppressed, with trifling blood-

shed.  At the same time the popular party in Upper Canada were led to venture on revolt, headed by a Scottish editor named Mackenzie. An attack was made by a disorderly body of the disaffected on Toronto, but it had no more effect than the rising in the lower province. The insurgent leaders who escaped death and capture succeeded in crossing the line into the United States.  Papineau and Mackenzie were both among the number.  Many of the rank and file of the insurgents also took refuge across the border, and found there a measure of sympathy and support that had serious consequences. For a year or more the Canadian frontier was harassed by a series of petty but exasperating raids organized and directed in the States of Vermont, New York, and Michigan.

The most important of these border forays was that conducted from Buffalo as a base in December, 1837.  A force of several hundred men took possession of an island on the Canadian side of the international boundary, as a first step toward attack on the mainland.  Supplies for the invaders were drawn from the American side by means of the small steamer *Caroline*.  Canadian troops, sent to destroy the steamer, found her lying at a wharf on the Amer-

ican shore, cut her loose, and burned her.  In
the slight skirmish that accompanied the seizure of the vessel an American was slain.  No
further progress was made by the invading
party on the island, but the destruction of the
*Caroline* by British troops in American territory
caused a fierce wave of indignation to sweep
through the United States.  To this incident,
more perhaps than to any other cause, was due
the prolongation of active movements against
Canada across the border.  Popular feeling was,
of course, no less wrathful on one side of the
boundary than on the other; for the Canadians
were deeply irritated at the sympathy and con-
nivance given by the Americans to the insurgents.

Diplomacy was prompt to take up the affair
of the *Caroline*, and urgent demands for reparation for the violation of American territory
were made by the United States upon the
British Government.  The latter assumed responsibility for the act as a regrettable but
necessary proceeding of defence in time of insurrection and flagrant war, during which the United
States was a base of supplies for the enemy.
Negotiations dragged according to their wont
until a fresh incident gave an exciting impulse

to their movement.  In November, 1840, three
years after the burning of the *Caroline*, Alexander McLeod, a British subject, was arrested in
New York State on a charge of arson and murder in connection with the affair.  Indignation
flamed high in Canada and Great Britain at
this action, and the authorities at Washington
were pressed to release McLeod, whose offence,
if any, had been committed as a soldier under
orders for which the British Government had
assumed responsibility.  The situation was most
difficult for the American Department of State;
for it involved an awkward conflict of jurisdiction, only too familiar, between the Federal
Government and the government of New York
State.  The latter, backed by a demonstrative
popular sentiment, insisted that its courts must
enforce its criminal law.  The right to do so
could not be questioned by the Federal Government, though the latter alone had to confront
the threatening demands of Great Britain for
the release of McLeod.  A way out was found
by Daniel Webster, who became secretary of
state in March, 1841.  He on the one hand
moderated the urgency of the British demands
and on the other moved all possible influences
to insure that McLeod should not be convicted

by the State court. In October the accused man was duly acquitted by a jury, and was hastily sent out of the State.

The period of McLeod's detention was one of great bitterness of feeling among all three of the English-speaking peoples. While exciting conditions of internal politics served to temper somewhat the prevailing international antipathies, there was little doubt that the gravest results would have followed the conviction and punishment of the man. The Canadian revolt was indeed only one of several matters that combined to produce the tension of the time. While the two Canadas were in the throes of civil war New Brunswick was on the verge of hostilities with the State of Maine over the old question of the disputed northeastern boundary. On the Gulf of Mexico Texas was fighting for independence from Mexico, and was receiving from sympathizers in the United States an amount and kind of assistance that had not been without effect on the expectations of the insurgent Canadians. Finally, on the far-distant Pacific coast the late thirties saw the beginning of an immigration from the United States into the valley of the Columbia River that foretold trouble over the Oregon country. The American people were indeed showing in every direction a disposition to burst the territorial bonds that confined them, easy as those bonds had been. And the far-flung interests of the British Empire need no more striking illustration than the fact that in whatever direction the Americans sought to expand their bounds, whether on the Atlantic or on the Pacific, in the Gulf of the tropics or under the Arctic circle, they found subjects of the Queen, with vested rights, opposing the movement.

The risings in Canada gave a healthy shock to British interest, which had been languid in respect to the American branch of the empire. Parliament, early in 1838, passed an act suspending the constitution of Lower Canada, and in the spring the Earl of Durham was sent out as governor-general, armed with dictatorial powers. His stay was short, but its influence was lasting; for it gave occasion for the famous report that furnished the mother country with her first clear ideas as to the causes, facts, and tendencies of the situation in North America. He showed that in every one of the North American provinces there was a standing political antagonism between the elected popular assembly and the executive officers appointed by the crown—such antagonism as had produced the revolution of 1688 in England and that of 1776 in America. This condition, dangerous everywhere, became disastrous in Lower Canada, where it brought to a head the race animosity that was the basis of all the trouble there. The general remedy for the evils concerned, in Lord Durham's opinion, was the introduction of responsible government, that is, responsibility of the executive to the representatives of the people in the assembly. As to the Canadas, his Lordship saw no hope of stability and peace save through the union of the two provinces under a single legislature and executive. By such a system the French element would be deprived of the hope of an independent, or at least autonomous, government, and the English-speaking people would be assured of the political predominance to which they were entitled by their numerical, economic, and intellectual superiority.

Lord Durham's outspoken project for submerging the French in Canada was equalled in candor by his discussion of the relations of the British provinces with the United States. The enterprise and material prosperity on the republican side of the boundary, as compared with conditions on the British side, he set forth in terms that were bitterly resented, especially in Upper Canada. He appraised in a spirit of judicial detachment the sympathy and support given by the people of the United States to the Canadian malcontents, and the expectations of the latter as to the possibilities of escape from British rule by incorporation into the republic. He estimated with care the strength of the traditional antipathy with which the aristocratic dominant class in Upper Canada regarded the democracy across the border. As against the force of this feeling he considered the influence that contiguity, with identity of problems and interests, would exert for the promotion of respect and amity. The general deduction from his calculation was that, in default of a very wise and considerate policy on the part of the home government, union with the United States might become a popular demand among both the French and the English elements in the Canadas.

The importance of Lord Durham's discussion of this point was conspicuous in view of ideas that were freely broached by British politicians of prominence at this time. A calculus of the value of colonies and dependencies was becoming a rather common feature of debate. Ultra Radicals like Roebuck and Hume, and less violent ones like Brougham, contended that the connection of the Canadas with Great Britain either already was, or in the near future would be, irrational and adverse to the true interests of both parties.  Cobden and his anti-Corn-Law followers assailed, in the name of economic and political liberty, the system under which, for the sake of imperial glory, the natural law of freedom in trade and navigation was set at naught.  Lord Durham himself had been identified with the Radicals, but on the question of colonies he did not join the ultras. The burden of his contention in his great report was, that the North American provinces should be so administered as to grow into a unified nationality, attached to the British Empire, and sharing by give and take in the civilization and progress of which that empire was the home.

Under an act of Parliament that went into effect in 1841 a new constitution for Canada became operative.  It joined the two provinces in a legislative union, with many features that Lord Durham had recommended.  The new system did not bring at once the tranquillity that had been hoped for.   It included, however, provisions through which the popular element in the legislature could grow in relative influence, and it became thus instrumental in the development of responsible government and an increasing autonomy.

Just at the time when the popular excitement along the border was at its height in connection with the insurrection in Canada, it was unfortunate, but scarcely surprising, that the friction over the unsettled boundary of Maine and New Brunswick should have become acute.   The King of the Netherlands had failed, as we have seen, to find any geographical facts that he would judicially warrant to embody the line described in the treaty of 1783.   After the failure of this arbitration, desultory negotiations were carried on by the two governments, but with little progress toward agreement;  so that in 1838 the "northwest angle of Nova Scotia" and the "highlands" were eluding the diplomats and surveyors as successfully as at any time during the previous half-century.   It had been informally agreed by the two governments that neither should seek to strengthen its position in the disputed territory pending the determination of the boundary.   Despite this agreement vexatious incidents occurred from time to time. The authorities of Maine and New Brunswick, while professing to conform with exactness to the agreement not to strengthen their respective positions, were at no less pains to see that their positions were not weakened. Settlers, both British and American, and for the most part of no very desirable character, drifted into the region; local officials of the neighboring jurisdictions extended their activities and arrested each other as intruders; lumbermen, with or without color of right, plied their enterprise in the rich forests of the no-man's-land. In the summer of 1838 an unusually large force of British lumbermen carried on extensive operations on the Aroostook River. Ordered off by an American official, they refused to go, and assembled in considerable numbers to maintain their position by force. The government of Maine thereupon sent a strong body of militia to enforce its authority, and the government of New Brunswick responded by procuring the despatch of a detachment of British regulars to the neighborhood.

No bloodshed resulted from this threatening situation. Popular and official excitement, of course, ran high along the border, and contributed to increase the wide-spread ill feeling already caused by the incidents of the rebellion in Canada. The British and American foreign offices quickly took charge of the affair and soothed the inflamed susceptibilities of Maine and New Brunswick. President Van Buren felt obliged to rebuke the rather high-handed way in which the governor of Maine had begun to make war on the British Empire. It was clear in this matter, however, as became even clearer a little later in the case of McLeod, that the constitutional partition of authority between the States and the Federal Government in the American system must often cause great embarrassment to the United States in its relations with foreign powers.

The most important practical result of this so-called "Aroostook war" was the impulse it gave to serious efforts toward the settlement of the boundary. Negotiations had lagged in a spiritless way ever since the failure of the arbitration. Maine was justified at least in her complaints on this score. The administrations of Jackson and Van Buren on the one side, and the cabinet of the Melbourne Whigs on the other, found subjects much more to their taste than the exhausted and exhausting question as

to where the northwest angle of eighteenth-
century Nova Scotia was situated. The governor of Maine, with his militia, stirred up the
diplomats as effectually as he did the lumbermen. Palmerston, the British foreign secretary, and Forsyth, the American secretary of
state, after some despatches manifesting more
acerbity than had characterized the correspondence since Canning's time, agreed in a recognition of each other's highly correct and amicable
intentions, and proceeded to institute a new
series of surveys and a new set of commissioners to guess out the location of the elusive
angle and highlands. For three years, 1839-42,
there was great activity in the search for the
boundary and vast ingenuity was displayed in
the construction of new theories about the meaning of the treaty and the topography of the disputed region. The country was so covered with
hills that a surveyor who knew it well could
construct a chain of highlands in nearly any
direction that suited his taste or his instructions, and was as free to indulge his fancy
about the boundary as were the negotiators
in 1783, who knew nothing whatever about the
facts.

In 1841 there was a change of administration

in both Great Britain and the United States.
At Washington in March the American Whigs
assumed control of the government; at London
in September the British Whigs fell from power.
Daniel Webster became American secretary of
state, and Lord Aberdeen became foreign secretary in place of Palmerston. The relations
of the English-speaking peoples with one another could scarcely have been more unpleasant
than they were at the time of these changes.
The McLeod incident, with the other friction
due to the Canadian insurrection, was at the
most critical stage, and the boundary dispute
was as far as ever from settlement. Added to
these came a fresh revival of the old and extremely inflammatory issue about the right of
search. Slave-traders of various nationalities
were freely using the American flag to protect
themselves, and British cruisers on the African
coast, in trying to stop the trade, now and then
visited and examined a vessel whose right to
carry the American flag was beyond question.
The complaints of merchants whose business
was thus interfered with led to energetic protests to the British Government, and one of the
last acts of Palmerston before his retirement
from the Foreign Office was to send in reply to

such a protest a despatch that raspingly refused
to concede the American demand.

With Aberdeen at the Foreign Office the tone
of the correspondence between the two governments underwent a notable change. Webster,
after seeing the McLeod affair peacefully settled, went earnestly to work on the boundary
question. His plan was to drop all the great
mass of surveyors' and historians' data, to give
up trying to find out the meaning of the treaty,
and to reach an agreement by direct negotiation on a conventional line. It was deemed
necessary first to obtain the assent of Maine
and of Massachusetts (within whose jurisdiction Maine was originally included) to this
method of settlement. Though the government of Maine had declared in the most formal
way that it would never consent, it consented,
and Massachusetts raised no difficulties. The
British Government showed its sense of the importance of the whole situation by announcing
that it would send a special envoy to deal with
the pending questions, and manifested its amicable spirit by designating for the mission
Alexander Baring, Lord Ashburton, whose fitness was signified equally by his distinguished
public services in England and his well-known

cordiality toward the United States. Ashburton reached Washington in April, 1842, and on the 9th of August the famous Webster-Ashburton treaty was signed. It was savagely attacked in the British provinces, in Great Britain itself, and in the United States. These attacks were for the most part, however, mere ebullitions of partisan spite or of that queer conception of public duty which requires fault to be found with every achievement of the administration for the time being.

So far as it went the Webster-Ashburton Treaty was an extremely important step in the development of pacific relations among the English-speaking peoples. The convention itself provided definitely a settlement of all open questions about the boundary from the Atlantic Ocean to the Rocky Mountains; it established an unobjectionable, if not supremely efficient, system of co-operation for the suppression of the slave-trade; and it embodied an agreement for the extradition of criminals that was urgently demanded by the disturbed conditions along the Canadian frontier. In the published correspondence between the negotiators were incorporated a satisfactory expression of regret by Great Britain for the violation of American ter-

ritory in the affair of the *Caroline,* and an exchange of views that was interpreted by Webster as a substantial abandonment of the ancient
claim to the right of search and impressment.
In regard to the case of McLeod, Webster renewed the admission by the United States of
the British contention that a private citizen
could not be punished for an act for which his
government assumed the responsibility, but
amicably forbore to point out, as his predecessor had done, the awkward position in which
the British Government would be put by this
contention in connection with certain incidents
of Palmerston's aggressive policy in the affairs of continental Europe.   The forbearance of
Webster in this matter was typical of the general tone of the correspondence and of the whole
negotiation.   A spirit of friendliness and courtesy was manifested at every stage, and an
almost ostentatious avoidance of ideas or expressions that could irritate.   Whatever of
soothing effect was produced by the mission of
Lord Ashburton was probably due as much to
this characteristic of the negotiations as to the
treaty itself.

   The boundary fixed by the treaty gave to
Maine a little more than half of the area claimed

by her, and a little less than what was assigned to her by the rejected arbitration of the King of the Netherlands. As a solace she received from the United States the sum of $150,000, a like sum going to Massachusetts. The line dividing Canada from Vermont and New York, which, as we have seen, had been erroneously run by the surveyors to the substantial advantage of the United States, was fixed by the treaty in accordance with the now long-established error.

The consent of Maine to the negotiation of a conventional line was secured largely through means that, when later disclosed, became the focus of a heated controversy. Just when Webster was getting his plans for the negotiation under headway his attention was called to a map recently discovered in the French archives which might be the one which Franklin was known to have sent to Vergennes in 1782 with the bounds of the United States, as agreed upon by the negotiators of the treaty of peace, marked upon it by a strong red line. The new-found map bore no evidence as to its identity, but the boundary of the United States was marked on it with a strong red line, and the line in the region of Maine followed very closely that claimed by the British as designated by the treaty of 1783. Webster showed a copy of this map to the governor of Maine, suggesting how awkward it would be to go into a new arbitration with the possibility that the map might come before the arbiter. Maine gave in her adhesion to the project of a conventional line. Webster refrained from showing the red-line map to Lord Ashburton, and further directed Everett, the minister at London, to abandon all searching for maps that might have been used in the negotiations of 1782–3.

Under all the circumstances, this abstention from further map-hunting was a dictate of elementary prudence. It was made ridiculous by what became known a little later. In the British Museum lay the actual map used in the negotiations of 1782 by Oswald, one of the British commissioners, and on this map the boundary agreed to was marked by a line that followed very closely what was claimed by the United States. If Everett had continued his search and happened upon this map, Webster's way with Great Britain, if not with Maine, would have been materially smoothed.

Neither the red-line map nor Oswald's map came forth from retirement till Webster and

Ashburton had concluded their treaty. Then, in connection with the debate in the Senate on the ratification, the fact of the discovery in Paris became public, and from this followed the disclosure of Oswald's map, which had been removed to the British Foreign Office. The opponents of the treaty found in these incidents good material for their attacks upon it. Webster was accused of trickery, and Ashburton of imbecility. The whimsical fortune that gave to each party exclusive control of evidence strongly sustaining its adversary made the situation most interesting, and promoted a diligent re-examination of the boundary issue on its merits. A furious cartographic controversy developed, in official and non-official circles. Maps, rumors of maps, traditions of maps, bearing on the line described in the treaty of 1783, came forth in impressive but perplexing numbers. Long before the debate assumed its greatest dimensions, however, the treaty of 1842 was duly ratified. To the layman the arguments of the cartographic and historical experts were reciprocally annihilating, and the wisdom of the negotiators in discarding the whole method was confirmed. All of ill feeling from the treaty that survived into later years was that on the part of the British-Americans, who were debarred by the Webster-Ashburton boundary from the most direct and practicable line of communication between Halifax and Quebec. They long continued to feel that their interests and plain rights had been sacrificed to the mother-country's exaggerated fear of a breach with the United States.

The provisions of the treaty touching the slave-trade avoided all reference to the right of search. It was agreed that each government should maintain on the coast of Africa a considerable naval force to apply its own laws against the trade. The two forces were to work in co-operation with each other for the common end, under orders from their respective governments adapted to make this co-operation most effective.

This article was the best that could be devised to end the dangerous controversies that arose from time to time over the activities of the British cruisers on the African coast. It insured a more positive and definite participation by the United States in the suppression of the slave-trade, and at the same time, by providing for the presence of an American squadron in the most troublesome neighborhood, gave some guarantee that slavers who misused the flag and traders who lawfully used it should be judged by its natural protectors rather than by the officers of a foreign power. The article in this shape was designed to leave wholly untouched the controversy over the right of search, and merely to reduce the frequency of the incidents that might raise anew that controversy.

At this date the discussion of the right of search by the publicists, official and unofficial, had assumed new phases in connection with the matter of the slave-trade. How, it was asked, could the nefarious traffic ever be interfered with, if a vessel loaded with slaves could escape examination by the simple expedient of running up a flag other than that of the cruiser that wished to examine her? There must be at least such examination as will determine whether the suspected ship has a right to the colors which she displays. Irrespective, thus, of any serious *search*, there must be a right of *visitation* as to a merchantman concerning which there is any ground for suspicion.

Not so, was the reply. Visitation would be futile without such a degree of examination as would constitute all that is involved in the practice of search. The claim of the lesser right is no more tenable in law and reason than the ancient pretension to the greater. The utmost that can be conceded is the right of *approach*. A cruiser may regard from a respectful distance and in a peaceful manner a ship flying an innocent flag, but any attempt by force to stop such a ship or to interfere with her course is a violation of the flag and of that freedom of the seas on which the civilization and progress of mankind so closely depend.

But what if the suspected vessel is a pirate? Shall a pirate be allowed to roam the seas at will, guaranteed against interference by the possession of a few lockers full of flags that she has taken from the victims of her lawlessness? Far from it, was the answer. A pirate has been from time immemorial, under the law of nations, *hostis humani generis*—at war with all mankind. No one pretends that the right of search is not possessed by a belligerent in time of war, as a reasonable precaution against the rendering of aid to the enemy. Only in time of peace is it wholly without justification. But as to pirates there is never a time of peace. War is permanent and coextensive with the human race. Therefore, as to pirates the right of search on the high seas belongs to the ships of all nations at all times.

These various arguments were iterated and reiterated, amplified and fortified with the ingenuity and historical learning that the experts in diplomacy and international law were readily able to supply. The practical outcome so far as concerned Great Britain and America was determined, however, by popular feelings that were independent of the reasoning on abstract principles. In the United Kingdom the humanitarian sentiment against the slave-trade pervaded all classes and demanded insistently that the great naval power of the government should be freely used for the suppression of the evil. In the United States the memory of conditions during the Napoleonic wars was unceasingly active and prohibited any semblance of recognition to the exercise of British jurisdiction for any purpose on American vessels on the high seas. There was a wide-spread belief in the United States that the British enthusiasm for the suppression of the slave-trade covered a greater enthusiasm for maintaining the right of search as the unmistakable token of her naval supremacy. Nor was this belief without foundation; for in some centres

of surviving high Toryism the sufferings of the
Africans were notoriously of little concern in
comparison with the maintenance intact of
British rule on the seas as against the aspirations of the upstart republic of the West. On
the other hand, there was a feeling among the
liberals in England that the obstinate refusal
of the Americans to join with whole soul in the
operations against the slavers was dictated less
by fears and scruples about the right of search
than by unavowed indifference to the existence
of the traffic. And this again was not without
foundation; for the trend of events during the
past ten years in relation to slavery had markedly
strengthened a feeling in the South that war
on the slave-trade was too closely associated
with abolitionism to be wholly free from peril
to the institutions of the section.

In the negotiations of 1842 Webster secured
an opportunity to put his government's views
correctly on the record, by asking that the right
of search in connection with impressment, rather
than with the slave-trade, be taken up for discussion. Ashburton declared that his instructions did not permit him to enter upon that
subject. Webster made use of the occasion to
enlarge with eloquence and force upon the views

of his government. The most significant feature of his plea was probably not his solemn
declaration that the United States would no
longer permit the impressment of seamen from
American vessels, but the attention that he
gave to the remarkable change of conditions
since the practice was last resorted to. He ad-
verted to the extraordinary proportions attained by immigration from the British Isles,
much of it encouraged by the British Government, and he pointed out the disastrous consequences that would ensue if, in time of future
war, any attempt should be made to assert the
doctrine of indefeasible allegiance among these
swarming myriads and to force them into the
service of the government that had encouraged
them to leave its soil.

Ashburton's answer was of the soft species
that turneth away wrath. He declined to enter
into argument and merely deprecated the discussion of a topic that was so full of difficulty
in the abstract and so happily remote from any
practical importance. He freely admitted, however, that a serious question "has existed, from
practices formerly attending the mode of manning the British navy in times of war." This
form of expression indicated a belief that impressment was a matter of the past.

It is not unlikely that Webster, when inject-
ing the discussion of impressment into the correspondence with Ashburton, was conscious of
the influence it might have as a set-off against
the attacks of the anti-slavery agitators upon
the United States. In America, at least, forced
service in the navy was regarded as not much
different in principle from forced service in the
cotton-field. So long as the British Government insisted on the right to drag freemen away
into such servitude, its interest in mitigating
the woes of the African slave savored of hypoc-
risy. The utility, if not the validity, of this
kind of reasoning was rendered obvious by an
incident that threatened serious consequences
just at the time of the Webster-Ashburton negotiations.

In November, 1841, the brig *Creole* was
bound from Hampton Roads to New Orleans
with a few passengers and 135 slaves on board.
On the way the slaves rose in revolt, slew one
of the passengers, wounded many of the crew,
and took the vessel into the British port of
Nassau, in the Bahamas, where the local authorities, after arresting those of the slaves who
were implicated in the mutiny, forcibly took the
rest from the ship and set them free. This

action caused intense exasperation in the United
States, especially in the South. The feeling
was not softened by the fact that Northern
abolitionists rapturously applauded the freeing of the slaves. The case was indeed only
the culmination of a series in which, since the
emancipation of the blacks in the West Indies,
the Bahama officials had rigorously applied the
principle of English law that a slave on entering the jurisdiction of Great Britain became
*ipso facto* free. Webster felt obliged to inject
this matter also into the correspondence with
Lord Ashburton, contending that under the
law of nations jurisdiction over a foreign ship
brought into a port against its will did not
extend to the divesting of property rights on
board, and that on the general principles of
international comity rigorous procedure under
such circumstances as those that brought the
*Creole* into port was barbarous, and destructive
to all hope of amicable relations. Here again
Ashburton disclaimed authority to go at large
into the question, but engaged that the governors of the British colonies near the slave States
should be cautioned against "officious interference with American vessels driven by accident
or by violence into those ports."

The pacific adjustment of the boundary on the northeastern border of the United States was the most decisive and satisfactory feature of the treaty. There had been high hopes in British governmental circles that all the old questions at issue between the two nations would be set at rest. Not only did these hopes fail, but almost before the ink was dry on the treaty the unsettled issues took on a threatening aspect. American aspirations were directed with new earnestness to territorial expansion on the Gulf of Mexico and on the Pacific Ocean. British interests were supposed to require that such expansion should be thwarted. Out of this situation arose serious ill feeling, both governmental and popular, in relation to Texas, Oregon, and California.

Texas was in 1842 an independent republic, recognized as such by the leading powers of the world, though not by Mexico. British interests in Mexico were very large, chiefly through the extensive holdings of Mexican bonds in Great Britain. Texas freed herself from Mexican rule in the later thirties, largely through the aid given by immigrants and adventurers from the United States. The British Government at first used its influence to bring about the reunion of the revolted state to Mexico. In 1839, however, the policy was changed, and systematic pressure was brought to bear to induce Mexico to recognize the independence of Texas. Palmerston, then at the British Foreign Office, was convinced that the Texans were too strong to be reconquered, and that further efforts in that direction would only bring the Americans in overwhelming numbers to the aid of Texas, with annexation to the United States as the inevitable result. For Mexican welfare it was important, he argued, that there should be a strong buffer state to hold the ever-aggressive Americans in check. For British interests a great cotton-growing community, competing with the United States, promised signal advantages in commerce and industry. This reasoning failed to win Mexico, and Great Britain, abandoning the hope of harmony with the Mexican Government, conceded the long-withheld recognition of Texan independence.

The treaties that embodied this recognition were ratified only in the middle of 1842. One of them was directed to the suppression of the slave-trade through the reciprocal grant of the right of search. The first diplomatic representative sent by Great Britain to Texas was an

ardent abolitionist, who began unofficial efforts to bring about the emancipation of the
slaves in Texas through money loaned by Great
Britain. Thus there entered into the situation
an influence that was destined to have most
important consequences. In the course of 1843
Lord Aberdeen committed his government definitely to the policy of promoting abolition
in Texas. Reports of this proceeding, however
inaccurate and distorted, produced an immediate commotion in the United States. That
Great Britain should be taking any active interest whatever in Texan affairs, was regarded
all over the land as disquieting; that she should
be seeking to abolitionize Texas, was regarded by
the slave States as a malicious attack on their
welfare. The long-dormant project of annexation was taken up and pressed with energy as
the only sure way of counteracting the insidious
activity of the British. Not that Aberdeen's
policy was the sole basis of the new agitation;
but it played an important part in the affair
and revealed again the peculiar sensitiveness of
the Americans in relation to Great Britain.

Advances to Texas in respect to annexation
were made by the United States in the autumn
of 1843, and a treaty was concluded in April of

1844. Two months later the treaty, after a fierce struggle, was rejected by the American Senate. During this whole period the British Government, as is known perfectly now but was only a matter of strong suspicion at the time, labored earnestly to thwart annexation. Aberdeen sought the support of France and proposed to Mexico that, if she would recognize the independence of Texas, Great Britain and France should jointly guarantee the boundaries of both Mexico and Texas against the United States. This drastic project was eventually dropped because France declined to face a war with the United States, and because the British and French ministers at Washington agreed in reporting that the immediate result, if the plan should become known, would be the carrying out of annexation at all hazards by the United States. In the presidential campaign of 1844 a demand for annexation was formally incorporated into the platform of the Democratic Party, and that party triumphed in the election. British "interference" in American affairs was a conspicuous theme of Democratic denunciation during the heat of the canvass, and the suspicions, half-truths, and downright fabrications that always play so large a part on such occasions evoked abundant manifestations of anti-British feeling among the people. Under the impulse of the Democratic victory President Tyler pressed upon Congress a plan for the annexation of Texas by legislative act rather than by treaty, and the plan was adopted in the ensuing session and put in operation by Tyler before the inauguration of the newly elected President, Polk. The formal consummation of the plan was effected by the latter late in 1845. Aberdeen's efforts to thwart it did not cease till the decisive step toward entering the Union was definitely taken by Texas itself.

Meanwhile a more open and dangerous controversy with the United States had developed in relation to the interests of the two nations in the Oregon country. The region concerned lay between the Pacific Ocean and the Rocky Mountains and between the parallels of 42° and 54° 40′ north latitude. Under the treaties of 1818 and 1827, as we have seen, the boundary in this region was left undetermined, and the country was left "free and open . . . to the vessels, citizens and subjects of the two Powers." The object of this provision was to permit the natural course of settlement to proceed without interference and furnish some indication of a desirable boundary. British occupation was carried out by the Hudson's Bay Company, which established a chain of posts along the Columbia River from the ocean to the mountains, with other posts to the northward and the southward. This famous company absorbed in 1821 its rival, the Northwest Company, of Montreal, and thereafter possessed a monopoly of all trade throughout British America to the west and north of Canada. Of government for this vast territory there was none save that furnished by the agents of the company. As a commercial enterprise the company was successful. As a promoter of colonization it was worse than useless. Its interest lay obviously in maintaining the conditions that produced the most furs; settlements and civilization were not among such conditions. Hence all the reports and all the influence of the great company were strongly adverse to any influx of settlers either overland from the provinces or by way of the ocean.

American occupation of the Oregon territory began with the establishment of Astoria as a fur-trading post at the mouth of the Columbia just before the War of 1812. Seized by the

British during the war, it was restored in accordance with the terms of peace, but was
ultimately abandoned by the American traders.
During the twenties the fur-trade that centred
in Saint Louis extended its operations on a
large scale beyond the Rocky Mountains. The
South Pass, through which the first transcontinental railway was destined to cross the mountains, was discovered and was made the high-
way for a well-organized traffic with the Indians
and trappers in the extreme southeastern part
of the Oregon territory. From the South Pass
access to the head-waters of the Columbia River
was, by the standards of that vast wilderness,
short and easy. Hence communication with
the Hudson's Bay Company's posts soon became frequent, and the famous Oregon Trail
entered into history.

Early in the thirties futile schemes for emigration to Oregon were essayed by restless and
visionary New Englanders. Somewhat later a
definite impulse to interest in the region was
given by the missionary spirit of the Methodists
and Presbyterians. Parties sent out under the
auspices of these sects in 1834 and succeeding
years crossed the plains and the mountains in
company with the fur-traders who set out in

well-organized caravans from Saint Louis every spring. The purpose of the missionaries was to Christianize and civilize the Indians, but the sites selected for the stations were naturally determined by the requirements of the white man's life. The valleys of the Columbia and its tributaries were found to abound in rich agricultural lands. The climate was mild and the rainfall copious. Reports of the attractiveness of the region circulated through the United States, together with highly colored descriptions of the establishments by which the Hudson's Bay Company was maintaining and consolidating the British occupation. As a consequence demands began to be heard, in Congress and out, for action by the government for the encouragement and protection of an American occupation. Before anything was done, however, emigration from the settled States assumed large proportions. From 1841 every spring saw a numerous company start from western Missouri on the long journey to Oregon, which they were lucky to reach six months later. Arrived in the promised land, they found no semblance of political organization or authority save where the British flag waved over the posts of the Hudson's Bay Company.

Resentment at such a condition of affairs was expressed with steadily increasing volume throughout the United States, but especially in the West, and was accompanied by shrill demands that the American claim to the whole of the Oregon territory should be effectively asserted. In the presidential campaign of 1844 the Democrats united this demand with that for the annexation of Texas. "Fifty-four forty or fight" was the alliterative slogan that embodied the jingoistic feeling as to Oregon. The Democratic convention recorded in the party platform its conviction "that our title to the whole of the territory of Oregon is clear and unquestionable; that no portion of the same ought to be ceded to England or any other power." With all due allowance for the insincerities and bluster of campaign declamation, the election of Polk on such a platform, together with the popular feeling exhibited during the canvass, gave strong evidence that the time was at hand for a definitive settlement of the long-standing question. The inaugural address of the new President, in March, 1845, made the matter perfectly clear. Polk declared it his duty to "assert and maintain by all constitutional means the right of the United States to that portion of our territory which lies beyond the Rocky Mountains." This declaration attracted much attention in Great Britain, where it was regarded as a bellicose claim to the whole of Oregon. Sir Robert Peel, the prime minister, as well as the leader of the opposition and other political chieftains, felt called upon to make public counter-declarations that British claims to the region would be sustained at all hazards.

While this little flurry of long-range defiance was in progress, with the embellishments that the newspapers were able to add, a more significant element in the general situation showed itself in the unusually large numbers that assembled in western Missouri to join the annual trek over the Oregon Trail. The character of these emigrants was as a whole excellent, and their purpose of making homes for themselves in the distant territory was guaranteed by the large numbers of women and children in every party. To look after the interests of these people, both on their long progress across the plains and mountains and in their new homes, was a most obvious duty of a government that made any pretensions to efficiency.

Polk's secretary of state, Buchanan, took up

the Oregon question with Pakenham, the British minister at Washington, in the summer of 1845. Negotiations as to the northwestern boundary of the United States had been carried on at intervals ever since the purchase of the Louisiana territory in 1803 gave the United States a definite interest in the region. Diplomacy had exhausted all the arguments based on discovery, exploration, treaty, and occupation, without leaving any possibility that either the British or the American Government could exclude the other entirely from the tract in dispute. Division of the territory had been proposed by both sides, the Americans offering the extension of the parallel of forty-nine degrees from the Rocky Mountains to the Pacific, the British insisting on the Columbia River from the point at which its northern branch was intersected by the same parallel. Near the close of Tyler's administration an offer of arbitration by the British was declined. When Buchanan resumed negotiations in July, 1845, he again offered forty-nine degrees to the Pacific, explaining that while President Polk believed the American claim to the whole region was valid, he felt precluded by the acts of his predecessors from insisting on it without first trying what they had been willing to concede. Pakenham here made a grave tactical error. Without consulting his government he rejected the proposal, in terms so peremptory and ill-advised as to give great offence to the President. Polk promptly revealed a spirit that he had not been supposed to possess. Against the almost tearful protests of the timid Buchanan he practically broke off negotiations by directing the secretary to withdraw his offer and to refrain from all further consideration of the question until some definite proposal should be received from Great Britain. This position the President maintained unflinchingly despite repeated efforts of Pakenham to induce a renewal of the offer; for Lord Aberdeen had disapproved of his course in rejecting it, and Pakenham was left in a very uncomfortable position.

In his message to Congress in December, 1845, Polk confirmed his uncompromising attitude by revealing the whole situation, claiming that the conciliatory policy of the United States had been flouted by Great Britain, and calling upon Congress for legislation to sustain the right to all Oregon, and to protect its citizens who should settle therein. As against the policy of Great Britain he propounded two dogmas that must prevail in relation to America: first, that there must be no interference by European powers with the independent action of the nations on this continent; second, that no new colony shall be established by any European power in North America. These principles he considered to be implicit in the celebrated dicta of President Monroe twenty-two years earlier, which he cited and reaffirmed. Polk's immediate application of his principles was, of course, to Texas and Oregon. If any portion of the people of this continent should wish to join with the United States, no European power shall interfere to prevent the union; further, "no future European colony *or dominion* shall, with our consent, be planted or established on any part of the North American continent." As the first of these expressions referred unmistakably to Aberdeen's diplomatic activities in Texas, so the second, through the indefinite extension of Monroe's doctrine implied in the words I have italicized, referred no less clearly to Oregon.

This belligerent pronouncement of Polk was naturally the prelude to a long season of warlike feeling and hostile recrimination on both sides of the Atlantic. As the treaty of 1827 provided for the termination of the joint occupation of Oregon by one year's notice from either government, Polk asked Congress for authority to give the necessary notice. After debates lasting all through the winter, the authority was given, and Great Britain was duly notified in April of 1846. Long before this date, however, a way had been found for the resumption of diplomatic discussion of the question. Polk stiffly maintained his old position, but consented to take the advice of the Senate on any proposal that should come from Great Britain. The offer duly came of the forty-ninth parallel, reserving to the British Vancouver Island and the navigation of the Columbia River. On the advice of the Senate Polk accepted this; the treaty was signed June 15, 1846, and went into effect in August. This happy outcome not only ended a dangerous tension between the two great English-speaking peoples, but by completing a conventionally fixed boundary from ocean to ocean, seemed to remove definitively a prolific source of controversy. Unfortunately a small fraction of the line at the ocean end was defined in terms of geography rather than astronomy, and thus a dispute was prepared that was destined to carry the history of boundary troubles over another quarter of a century.

Before a settlement was reached of this rather insignificant difficulty Alaska had been acquired by the United States, with additional thousands of miles of contact with British territory, and material was provided for controversy that extended well into the twentieth century.

When the Oregon dispute was ended by the signing of the treaty, the United States was at war with Mexico. Hostilities had been precipitated by a collision between Mexican and American troops on territory claimed by both governments. War had been practically certain ever since the annexation of Texas, and Polk was on the point of beginning it on other grounds when the destruction of a small detachment of American troops gave him an opportunity to appeal strongly to popular passion. The grievances of the United States against Mexico were neither new nor few, but it was well understood that they could be satisfactorily adjusted by a cession of territory. California, extending some ten degrees of latitude southward from Oregon on the Pacific coast, was on the point of revolt from the weak and distant central government of Mexico. That the Californians were in mortal terror of the Yankees was common knowledge; that British relations with Mexico were

intimate was equally well known. The pre-
dilection of Great Britain for coastal territory
all over the globe, especially where adorned
with so attractive a harbor as that of San Fran-
cisco, had been exhibited for centuries. Finally,
the British naval squadron on the Pacific coast
displayed from time to time a kind and degree
of activity that aroused grave suspicions of sinister designs. Out of all these elements was
developed a wide-spread belief in the United
States that California was about to fall into the
hands of Great Britain. While the Oregon
issue was acute, this feeling was naturally a
source of much unhappiness. Polk entered the
White House with a firm purpose to settle for
all time the California question by acquiring the
territory, with such an additional tract in the
interior as would neatly round out the boundary eastward to Texas. Since Mexico refused
to listen to any proposition for the purchase of
California, forcible acquisition became an indispensable feature of Polk's programme, and
the Mexican War would doubtless have taken
place regardless of all other matters at issue.

What actual ground there was for the fear
that Great Britain was seeking to forestall America in California has become known only in re-

cent years. The gist of Lord Aberdeen's policy was, not to acquire California for Great Britain, but to keep it out of the hands of the United States by any means short of war. His position was the same as in relation to Texas. The interests of Great Britain required that the expansion of the American Republic be opposed by every peaceful influence. Aberdeen would have guaranteed California to Mexico if France had been willing to join in the bond. He rejected overtures from a revolutionary party of California who suggested a British protectorate, but accompanied the rejection with a plain intimation that if a revolt should separate the province from Mexico, Great Britain would prefer to give it protection rather than see that function undertaken by any other power. After the annexation of Texas, when war was clearly impending, he urged Mexico in the most energetic terms to avoid war, on the ground that she would surely lose California also. He even took into apparently serious consideration schemes for the creation of a British interest in California by large grants of land to British holders of Mexican bonds. But this was at the time when the Oregon question was in its acute stage, and the British cabinet perceived easily enough that any such proceeding would be regarded as hostile by the United States, and would indefinitely postpone the settlement that was so eagerly desired. To keep open the possibility of Mexican aid in case the Oregon dispute led to war, was a most obvious duty of the British Government, and accordingly Aberdeen continued to show interest in California in the winter of 1845-46. After the way to agreement with the United States became clear, and Mexico at the same time took the course that made a breach with that nation certain, California and Mexico were both left to their fate.

If reason were anything like as large a factor in human affairs as is often pretended, the friction between Great Britain and the United States in the forties over Oregon and California, if not over Texas, would never have developed. There was nothing of the rational in the spirit that led the American immigrants to Oregon, when much more promising opportunities for welfare in every sense lay open without a journey of two thousand desert miles to reach them. The acquisition of California was projected before any man faintly suspected its power to satisfy the hunger for gold, and when its enormous area could not reasonably be expected to

be adequately peopled for centuries.  So far as
suspicion of British designs on the Pacific territory operated to promote the American policy,
that policy was doubtless rational;  for the history of the British Empire gave little assurance
of a dislike for expansion, and strong Britain
would be a less desirable neighbor than weak
Mexico.  Yet it would not have been difficult to
ascertain and publish the truth, that neither the
government nor the people of Great Britain in
the forties had any wish or purpose to acquire
any regions contiguous to the United States.
The rather pronounced trend of feeling was in
just the opposite direction, toward the thought
that there was already somewhat more contact with the republic than was altogether desirable.

What did most to increase by two-thirds the
already vast area of the United States was the
aggressive idealism of the American democracy.
In the forties this characteristic was probably
at its maximum.  The nation was permeated
with a sense of power and of destiny that tolerated no suggestion of limit in any direction.
On the cultural side indications of an approaching realization of the ideal were scanty;  on the
material side every manifestation of bigness

was accepted as normal and inevitable. The addition of 12,000,000 square miles of territory to their 18,000,000 aroused no misgivings in the mass of the people, and there were not lacking those who felt that the whole of Mexico should properly have been taken over instead of the northern provinces only. In the very month in which the treaty of peace was signed (February, 1848), by one of the most astonishing coincidences that history records, the acquisition of California was justified, in the economic sense, by the discovery of gold in its mountains. As against this providential confirmation of manifest destiny, promptly developed the bitter strife over slavery in the new territory, with results so disastrous to the unity of the nation.

Between 1815 and 1840 the population of the United States increased from 8,000,000 to 17,000,000. While large, this gain was not astounding, and it certainly gave no basis for an extension of territory. Overcrowding could not be considered imminent when the number of persons per square mile stood at 9.73. As compared with the United Kingdom the growth of the United States had effected a significant change in relations. The War of 1812 was fought by a people numbering 8,000,000 against one numbering 19,000,000; a war over Oregon would have pitted 20,000,000 against less than 27,000,000. What these figures portended as to the future distribution of the English-speaking race, was not difficult to see. With all its growth, however, whether absolute or relative, the American people sprawled and straggled over a territory much too large for its immediate needs, yet drew from the excess only the insatiable yearning for more.

In the thick of the unpleasantness over the Oregon question, it was often proclaimed by boastful Americans that Great Britain would not dare to fight a people so numerous as they had now become. So far as military or naval considerations were concerned, this was, of course, ridiculous. In another aspect, however, the growth of population in America had indeed raised up a powerful influence against war. British industry and commerce had become dependent in an extraordinary degree for their prosperity on the United States. As regularly as the seasons, three-fourths of the great cotton crop took ship for England from the ports of the southern States of the Union. Lancashire in the forties well understood the danger, that in the sixties became disaster, from the shutting off of the raw material for the cotton-mills. At the earlier date, moreover, the peril was greater; for as yet Great Britain was still feeding her people from her own crops, and the people often went hungry. Starvation on a large scale would have ensued very promptly if the cotton supply had been stopped in the early forties.

This was one disturbing result of the growth of population in the United Kingdom—a result that had no parallel in the United States. Where the food supply was redundant and cheap any interruption of normal economic processes by war or other disaster produced loss and discomfort but not famine. Where, as in England and Ireland, the food supply was precarious and dear, any interference with the normal conditions brought famine and revolt. In the early forties recurring distress and agitation among the working classes gave abundant warning to the leading statesmen that so grave an economic disturbance as would be involved in a war with the United States was not to be risked so long as any way of escape was open.

The task of handling the delicate issues that were presented by the international and the internal problems that have been noticed fell

to the lot of the Tory cabinet of Sir Robert
Peel, 1841–6. As the one set of problems centred in the due recognition of the American
democracy, so the other set involved large concessions to the democratic movement in Great
Britain. There was a connection between the
two that, while it did not escape notice in the
reasoned debates, for the most part lurked obscurely in the channels of popular feeling.
Peel's government was called upon to deal with
two questions of internal politics that particularly appealed to the American interest. These
were the repeal of the union with Ireland and
the abolition of the Corn Laws.

O'Connell's tremendous agitation for the restoration of an Irish Parliament such as had
existed before 1800, won sympathy in America
on various grounds other than that unthinking
joy which greeted every situation producing
trouble for the British Government. It seemed
to be the demand of the common people for
relief from oppression by a privileged class; it
seemed to be a demand for self-government as
opposed to foreign rule; it seemed to be a perfect application of that principle of nationality
that had been so eloquently proclaimed by
Englishmen, both official and unofficial, in sus-

taining the claims of the Greeks and the Poles
to independence. There survived, too, in the
United States, the tradition of Grattan's Parliament, which received the breath of life
through the success of the war that made
America free from Great Britain. Irishmen in
thousands, many of them high in the esteem of
their communities, pervaded the United States,
and preached antipathy to Britain. Repeal
rent, as the funds were called that sustained
O'Connell's cause, flowed in copious streams
from America. The suppression of the agitation by main force in 1843 made on more than
Irish hearts the impression that in the government of Peel the hated forces of aristocratic
tyranny were still clearly in the ascendant.

The different outcome of the popular movement against the Corn Laws in England had some
effect in moderating the distrust of Peel. When
he came to power in 1841, every branch of
British industry, mining, manufacturing, and
agricultural, was protected by customs duties.
When he left office five years later, the whole
protective tariff had disappeared, and Great
Britain was committed to freedom of trade.
This great revolution was a direct continuation
of the liberalizing reforms that had been in

progress since 1815. The immediate occasion
for the change was the necessity of readjustment
in the budget to get rid of a persistent deficit;
the character of the change was determined,
however, by the intellectual conviction slowly
reached by Peel and his coadjutors that Adam
Smith's economic philosophy was sound. To
get rid of the protection on manufactures was
no hard matter. The manufacturing centres
were the abodes of Whigs and Radicals, and
Peel's Tory followers were not unwilling to see
them ruined. By 1845, through successive re-
ductions, most of the old tariff was gone. The
process involved some changes in the agricultural items and every step in this direction
caused frantic alarm among the landowning
aristocracy who furnished the bulk of the Tory
party. It was becoming clear that the Corn
Laws were doomed, and it seemed likely that the
Tory leader himself was to be the agent for
executing the decree. The full meaning of this
situation to the aristocracy is to be realized
only when attention is given to the extra-
Parliamentary activities of the Anti-Corn-Law
League.

This organization was formed, as has been
stated, in the later thirties, and was made a

vital force by Richard Cobden.  In 1841 John
Bright became formally associated with Cobden
in their famous partnership of agitation.  Under
the leadership of these two men the League
was, in object, in methods, and in organization,
the open and determined foe of the ruling aristocracy.  Its members were drawn chiefly from
the working classes of the towns;  its branches
spread all over the land, on the model of the
associations which O'Connell had made so well
known;  its method was that of unceasing appeal, in speech and print, to the thought and
the emotions of the people;  its object was to
break down, not only the protective system and
its particular provision as to corn, but the whole
controlling influence of the landed aristocracy
in the public affairs of the British nation.
There was no effort to disguise this object.
Cobden's lucid reasoning was pointed with
scorn of the stupidity of the peers and squires
in failing to see that free trade in corn was
for their real interest;  Bright's passionate eloquence went straight to their selfishness, cruelty,
and oppression in fighting to keep up their
rents at the expense of a starving people.  A
stupid, selfish, cruel, tyrannical aristocracy, so
the corollary ran, must no longer control the

destinies of the nation.   The despised common
people  must  assert  themselves  and  be  free.
What Cobden and Bright did not say, though
the harried Tories were not silent about it, was
that the result of free trade would be to substi-
tute an industrial and commercial for the old
agricultural  aristocracy  in  dominion  over  the
nation.

From  1842  to  1845  bad  harvests,  industrial
depression, strikes, wide-spread poverty and distress in England played perfectly the game of
the Anti-Corn-Law League.   In the last of these
years came the frightful failure of the potato
crop, making imperative some drastic step to
mitigate the impending famine in Ireland.   Peel
knew that if he suspended the corn duties, as
had been done twenty years before in an emer-
gency, the League would be able to see to it
that they should never be restored.   He was
already convinced that protection was economically and politically wrong.   There was nothing for him to do but demand of his party
consent to the repeal of the Corn Laws.   His
measures for this purpose passed Parliament in
1846, but their passage was the death-knell of
the Tory party.   An embittered fraction of the
party, inspired chiefly by the rising Disraeli,

seized an early opportunity to desert the cabinet and effect its downfall.

The overthrow of the Peel government coincided in time with the conclusion of the treaty
settling the Oregon dispute. Aberdeen announced the agreement with the United States
to the House of Lords on the same day that his
retirement from office was announced. Though
Cobden and Bright, with their middle-class and
working-class followers, had played so large a
part in the politics that brought about the crisis,
it was not for them to take up the responsibilities of government. The Whigs, under Lord
John Russell, assumed the governmental power,
with Lord Palmerston at the Foreign Office, and
with little indication that the democracy of England was becoming self-conscious and articulate.

For the first two years of its life the Russell
administration was absorbed in dealing with
the terrible conditions due to the potato blight.
Famine effectually solved the problems of over-
population in Ireland. At the same time it
brought confusion into the whole social and
political situation of the United Kingdom.
American interest in British conditions received
a great stimulus from the disaster in Ireland.
Generous sums of money and whole fleets of

food-laden ships testified to the impression made by the pitiable sufferings of the afflicted people. Then came the great movement of the stricken Irish to the land of plenty. While the South and the West watched with all-absorbing interest the gleams of smudgy glory from the war in Mexico, the eastern ports of the United States gave attention to the dismal myriads of half-starved Celts that poured in from distracted Erin. Economic, social, and political problems of many kinds promptly appeared in connection with the influx of aliens that assumed vast proportions first in 1847. The Irish were but the largest element in the immigration. Germans in large numbers also fled from the pinch of the potato famine. It was through the Irish, however, that a new and most important element was introduced into the relations among the English-speaking peoples. Canada and the other British provinces in America received no insignificant share of the immigration, with results that soon made themselves noticeable. Full half a century was destined to elapse before the impulse first given by the famine in Ireland ceased to be easily distinguishable among the factors determining Anglo-American relations.

# CHAPTER IV

## THROUGH THREEFOLD TENSION TO HARMONY

Philosophical historians warn us against over-emphasis on particular units of time or of space or of personality. To centre attention on a single date, a single place, a single individual, is to distort the truth and misrepresent the general movements of events. If disregard of this wise warning may ever be tolerated, a fair case for a free hand is presented by the year 1848 in the history of the United States and its relations with Great Britain. Even more narrowly the month of February in that year may be assigned to a position of unique significance. To that month belong, as we have seen, the definitive acquisition of vast Mexican territory by the signing of the treaty of peace, and the discovery of gold in the newly acquired region. In the same month Louis Philippe was dethroned by a revolution in France, and a popular agitation was engendered that swept over all central and western Europe. Monarchies disappeared. Republics and constitutions and bills of rights and new nationalities became the order of the day. An orgy of liberalism convulsed the Continent; even the United Kingdom felt the delirium, and was forced to deal with the Chartists demanding democracy and Young Ireland proclaiming itself a nation. When the tumult, after several feverish years, subsided, the most conspicuous result of it all was, oddly enough, the revived Napoleonic Empire in France. Less obvious, but not less influential in the long run on the history of human progress, was the host of exiles from the Continent who betook themselves to the lands of the English-speaking peoples. In particular, a great body of ardent, high-spirited, but bitterly disappointed German liberals found refuge in the American Republic, in whose democratic institutions they expected to find a full realization of their cherished ideals. Though there was naturally much disillusionment when the actualities were discovered, the new environment did not fail to prove attractive, and these political exiles were followed by a stream of Germans rivalling in volume that which was flowing in full current from Ireland.

In Great Britain the revolutionary tempest

on the Continent gave occasion for new and striking manifestations of the species of foreign policy that was already associated with the name of Lord Palmerston.  His Lordship's sympathy and support went out to those who felt themselves to be victims of oppression with a degree of vehemence and ostentation that varied directly as the square of their distance from London.  The Italians and the Magyars received strong encouragement in their efforts to escape from the Hapsburgs;  the French republicans were tolerated in freeing themselves from Louis Philippe, but were relegated to the clutches of Napoleon III with much satisfaction;  the English Chartists and the Irish Repealers were, of course, summarily suppressed.  Whatever the defects or inconsistencies of Palmerston's conduct of the Foreign Office, it was enthusiastically supported by British popular sentiment.  It appealed effectively to the jingoistic spirit of a generation that had known only "little wars."  It was aggressive, but with a strongly liberal leaning in the immediate ends in view;  its heaviest demonstrations were directed against the Russian Czar and the Austrian Emperor, whose sins with respect to their subjects were aggravated by a presumed hostility of a specially deadly character to British interests in the Orient.

The Palmerstonian policy and methods were most violently antagonized by the Manchester School, as Cobden, Bright, and their followers were called. It was the cardinal doctrine of this school that internal, not international, affairs furnished the proper field for governmental activity at this particular time; that the welfare of the people and the due course of foreign relations would be best promoted by the readjustment of taxation, expansion of trade and industry, and abstention from the waste of war and of armaments in preparation for war. The two theories as to the policy of the government came to a decisive issue in the House of Commons in the famous debate over Don Pacifico in the middle of 1850. Against an assault led by Disraeli, Gladstone, Peel, and Cobden, Palmerston defended himself in his most celebrated speech, won a decisive triumph in the vote of the House, and thus committed Great Britain to the policy associated with his name. Only a few months later his natural bumptiousness, accentuated doubtless by the sense of his great victory, brought him into conflict with his chief, Lord John Russell,

and with Majesty itself, with the result that
Palmerston was summarily dismissed from his
place. Even this severe experience did not
loosen his hold on popular admiration and sympathy. The Whigs could not carry on the government without him, and fell from power; the
Aberdeen coalition cabinet drifted into the
Crimean War through the force of the Palmerstonian influence, but failed to develop the
vigor that the situation required. In 1855,
sorely against her own wishes, but responsive
to an overwhelming popular demand, the Queen
summoned Palmerston himself to form a cabinet. For more than eight of the remaining
ten years of his life he was prime minister, and
British foreign relations were presumed to follow the lines associated with his name, though
actually his policy and methods were substantially modified in passing through the hands of
the foreign secretaries, Clarendon and Russell.

It was well for the cause of amity that Polk
and Palmerston did not synchronize more precisely in their political ascendancy. A serious
clash between the two would have meant
disaster. The crude and narrow Tennessee
Democrat offered a strange contrast to the
broad culture and long experience of the Brit-

ish aristocrat, but neither exceeded the other
in strength of conviction that his people had
the right and the duty of asserting itself in
the world without overscrupulous regard for
the rights and interests of other peoples. It
was well again that Palmerston's chosen field
for manifesting British power was the hemisphere from which Polk deliberately excluded
himself. If this division of territory had worked
both ways, some friction between the two great
promoters of Anglo-Saxon ideas might have
been avoided. Polk's hemisphere was too thoroughly permeated with British interests, however, to permit of any American development
without touching them. Though Palmerston's
personal concern about the Americans was of
the slightest, and he preserved to the end the
attitude of his early chief, Canning, in regarding the United States as a vexatious intruder
in the field of serious diplomacy, yet his spirit
was active in the subordinates who were on the
ground in America, and trouble was an early
result.

The disintegration of Mexico on its northern
frontier and the great southward stride of the
United States along the Gulf of Mexico and the
Pacific Ocean naturally excited the liveliest

interest in Latin America and the colonial West Indies. With California a part of the United States, the long-discussed projects of easy transit from ocean to ocean across Central America assumed immediate and pressing importance. The discovery of gold and the ensuing movement of fortune-hunters and settlers in myriads to the Pacific territory added a prodigious practical emphasis. Before this unforeseen climax appeared, however, both British and American diplomats had been diligently fishing in the murky waters of Latin-American politics for a controlling position in respect to any possible isthmian canal. In the early forties a British official formally asserted that the territory of the Mosquito Indians included the port of San Juan de Nicaragua, which would be the terminus of any canal that should be cut across Nicaragua. As the Mosquitos were held to be a kingdom under the protection of Great Britain, the bearing of the claim on their behalf was obvious. In 1848 the British officer came to San Juan with a war-ship, captured the Nicaraguan garrison, established a British garrison in possession, and changed the name of the port to Greytown. Meanwhile a group of islands off the coast, conveniently situated with reference to San Juan and claimed by Honduras, was also occupied by a British garrison.

In New Granada, at about the same time, the American *chargé d'affaires* displayed a like activity, and in 1846, without instructions, concluded with the government of that state a treaty of far-reaching importance. By its provisions the government and citizens of the United States and their property secured freedom of transit across the Isthmus of Panama in return for a guarantee by the United States of the neutrality of the isthmus, and the further guarantee of the sovereignty and property of New Granada in the said territory. This treaty remained pending in the Senate until after the British movements in Nicaragua in 1848. In June of that year the treaty, with the advice and consent of the Senate, was duly ratified.

With this favorable position secured in respect to the Panama route, the Polk administration directed its attention to the situation in the region of the Nicaragua route. A *chargé d'affaires* was sent to Central America to ascertain the condition of affairs. He readily obtained from the Nicaraguan Government, which was highly indignant at the activities of Great Britain, a

treaty giving to the United States the exclusive
right to construct a canal or railway through
Nicaragua, in return for the guarantee of her
just limits.   Mr. Hise, who negotiated this convention, was succeeded shortly afterward by
President Taylor's appointee, Mr. Squier, who
in September, 1849, concluded a treaty with
Honduras by which the island of Tigre, on the
Pacific coast, was ceded to the United States.
This island commanded the western end of the
Nicaraguan route as Greytown commanded the
eastern end.   Less than a month after the conclusion of this treaty, a British force took possession of Tigre.

The situation thus created was a decidedly
serious one.   If all the successive proceedings
had become public as they occurred, the two
great English-speaking peoples would doubtless
have been at each other's throats in short order.
But communication with Central America was
arduous and slow, and diplomacy was able
to smooth out the wrinkles in the situation
before the public was aware that they existed.
Clayton, the new secretary of state at Washington, was of pacific disposition, and President
Taylor had none of the aggressive propensities
of his predecessor.   Nor did Lord Palmerston

show any tendency to crabbedness, regarding
the whole matter probably as a tedious trifle.
The two governments promptly exchanged assurances that no occupation or colonization of
Central America was contemplated, and no
exclusive control of a railway or canal across
the isthmus.  Clayton, on his side, withheld
from the Senate the draft treaties of Hise and
Squier; Palmerston disavowed the seizure of
Tigre and ordered the garrison to be withdrawn.
In considerable haste, lest new tempests should
issue from the prolific storm-centre on the Carib-
bean, the representatives of the two governments at Washington then concluded the famous
but ill-fated treaty of Clayton and Bulwer,
signed April 19, 1850, and proclaimed in effect
July 5th.

The purpose of this convention, as defined
by its own provisions, was to promote the construction and maintenance of an interoceanic
canal by the Nicaragua route "for the benefit
of mankind, on equal terms to all."  The two
governments engaged never to obtain any exclusive control over such a canal, never to erect
fortifications or establish colonies in its vicinity,
never to use any relation of protection, alliance,
or intimacy with contiguous states for the pur-

pose of obtaining special privileges in the use of
the canal. The two powers further undertook
a joint guarantee of the neutrality of the canal,
and of its protection from interruption, seizure,
or unjust confiscation.

The amicable and benevolent spirit supposed
to be embodied in this treaty soon proved to
be illusory. Approval of its provisions in the
United States had been based in no small degree upon the impression that Great Britain
was bound by it to abandon all her pretensions
to a political foothold in Central America.
Article I declared that neither party would ever
"colonize or assume or exercise any dominion
over Nicaragua, Costa Rica, the Mosquito
coast or any part of Central America," or make
use of any protectorate or alliance for the purpose of colonizing or exercising dominion over
those same carefully specified regions. Under
what appeared to be the obvious intent of this
article, the withdrawal of the British from the
Mosquito coast was awaited with impatience
in America, but no indication of approaching
withdrawal appeared. On the contrary, the
islands off the coast were in 1851 formally organized as a crown colony of Great Britain,
thus giving permanence and solidity to an oc-

cupation which had hitherto seemed tentative. Eventually it came to public knowledge, what the foreign offices had known only too well, that the British interpretation of the Clayton-Bulwer Treaty involved no obligation whatever to withdraw from Central America. The two governments were, in fact, seriously at logger-heads as to the meaning of the vaunted agreement.

The British position was this. Just prior to ratifying the treaty Sir Henry Bulwer, the negotiator, made the formal declaration that the British Government did not understand that the provisions applied to her Majesty's settlement at Honduras or to its dependencies. Clayton declared in reply that he also understood that Article I did not apply to "the British settlement in Honduras (commonly called British Honduras, as distinct from the State of Honduras), nor the small islands in the neighborhood of that settlement which may be known as its dependencies." The guarded expression of Clayton indicates the gist of the controversy that developed. Great Britain claimed a boundary for British Honduras, or Belize, as it was commonly called, that was denied by the Central American states; she claimed further that

the islands which had been made a colony were
dependencies of Belize; and she claimed finally
that the Clayton-Bulwer Treaty required her,
not to relinquish her protectorate over the
Mosquitos, but merely to abstain from using
this protectorate for the purpose of controlling the canal or of establishing colonies or
dominion in Central America. Any such purpose she categorically disclaimed. She early
manifested a readiness, moreover, to withdraw
from occupation of territory held in the name of
the King of the Mosquitos as soon as it should
appear that this humble potentate and his subjects were assured of proper respect by their
neighbors.

The American contention, as fully developed,
was based upon not only the Clayton-Bulwer
Treaty, but also the Monroe Doctrine. It denied the validity of any claim of sovereignty
by the Mosquitos, who, as a savage, degraded,
and insignificant tribe of Indians, could be
recognized by the public law of civilized nations as enjoying only a qualified right of occupation in the territory over which they roamed.
A "treaty" with such a tribe could not be regarded as vesting political authority in a great
power like Great Britain. The alleged "pro-

tectorate" was, therefore, the diplomatic equivalent of a fraud. As to Belize, history revealed that British rights there were limited to certain privileges of cutting mahogany and dye-woods, and included no political authority. This disposed of the claim to power over the adjacent islands as dependencies of British Honduras. The act of Great Britain in erecting these islands into a colony was therefore repugnant to the announcement of President Monroe, often since formally reiterated, that the United States could not recognize the American continents as open to colonization by European powers.

Controversy on the lines of these widely divergent views was active in diplomacy and in popular debate for many years. Greytown, or San Juan de Nicaragua, assumed much importance as a station on the route of the thousands who were seeking California. Americans in this adventurous host often took pains to show their disrespect for the officials who were exercising *de facto* authority there, and incidents occurred from time to time that caused popular indignation to flame high on both sides of the Atlantic. The troubles culminated in the bombardment and destruction of

Greytown by an American war-ship, as a punishment for violence by the townsmen to the American minister to Nicaragua.

James Buchanan went as minister to London in 1853 with the special mission of bringing the serious situation to a settlement. Under the pacific ministry of Lord Aberdeen it was not hard to reach the general outline of an adjustment. Great Britain was ready to relinquish the Mosquito protectorate and the Bay Island colony as soon as it could be done with grace and dignity. The peculiar politics of Nicaragua, with the extraordinary exploits of Walker's filibusters, interposed serious obstacles to this happy outcome, and the Crimean War raised up untimely diversion of the British Government's attention. Palmerston's accession to power in 1855 brought a noticeable stiffening up of the British attitude. In consequence Buchanan returned to America in the following year without his mission attained. As President of the United States, however, he was able to announce in his annual message of 1860 a final settlement of the subject in a manner entirely satisfactory to the United States.

The settlement in which Buchanan found reason for solid comfort was embodied in treaties

concluded by Great Britain in 1859 and 1860
with Honduras and Nicaragua respectively. In
these conventions all claim to a British protectorate over the Mosquito territory was relin-
quished and the sovereignty over that territory
within their respective frontiers was recognized
to the Central American states. The Bay
Islands were recognized as an integral part of
the republic of Honduras. In this adjustment
the contention of the United States as to the
effect of the Clayton-Bulwer Treaty was sustained in full. British Honduras was, indeed,
left to the dominion of Great Britain; but this
was in accordance with the view adopted by
the Americans that the territory was outside
of Central America, and therefore was not affected by the provisions of the treaty. So
far as concerned control over the expected
canal through Nicaragua, neither the United
States nor Great Britain had a privileged position in Central America. The great work
might, therefore, be expected to be brought to
completion promptly for the benefit of mankind. Unhappily, by the time when the way
became clear, all hope of progress in the actual
construction of the canal had been relegated to
an indefinitely distant future. Capital proved

less enthusiastic than diplomacy over the prospects of transisthmian communication; but, however slowly the realization of the great dream approached, and with whatever of wile and guile in the lobbies of legislation in Nicaragua and at Washington the realization must be promoted, the work of Clayton and Bulwer stood a majestic monument of a union of the two great English-speaking peoples for the accomplishment and protection of a great public work that should be "for the benefit of mankind, on equal terms to all."

While the tension over the Central American affairs was acute, its effect was aggravated by various other subjects of suspicion and of controversy between the two governments. The craving for expansion of territory continued to manifest itself in the United States and to take a form determined more or less by the sectional cleavage of the nation on the slavery question. There was a steady pressure from the southern States for the extension of influence and possessions in Latin America. Popular sympathy for the filibustering expeditions of Lopez against Cuba, and Walker in Central America, was strong enough to paralyze the efforts of the Washington government to prevent them. But the suggestion of a readiness on the part of Great Britain, in conjunction with her good ally Napoleon III, to undertake a guarantee of the threatened regions against the filibusters was peremptorily repelled by the United States. This much of interest in the subject by Great Britain only confirmed, however, the apprehensions of the extreme pro-slavery partisans in the South, to whom the avowed abolitionism of the British was an ever-present terror.

Internal party politics in the middle fifties contributed singularly to confirm the American manifestations of anti-British feeling. After 1852 the Democratic Party controlled the government. The strength of this party consisted largely of the slaveholders of the South and the masses of Irish immigrants in the North. Enmity toward all things British was a dominant passion in both these classes. That the administrations of Pierce and Buchanan should, under the circumstances, have preserved amity with Great Britain, is a tribute to the diplomatic correctness of statesmen whose reputations have been dimmed by the malevolence of later political events.

What was probably the most serious situation during the period we are discussing was produced by the Crimean War. The causes and issues of that strange conflict, grasped only with much difficulty by the experts in Europe, were quite unintelligible in the United States. Sufficient for general popular feeling was the fact that Great Britain was a party to the war, in which case the other party must be right. Such at least was the reasoning of an influential element of American society. It was ill-judged by the British Government that the time should have been selected for the project of raising a foreign legion in America to serve in the Crimea. The enlistment of troops for military service against a friendly power was, of course, prohibited by the laws of the United States. Success in the enforcement of the laws had not been especially marked in the case of the filibusters. Whether this fact was taken into account by the British, need not be debated. At all events, a systematic procedure was instituted through which a large number of men were forwarded from the United States to Halifax, to be there regularly incorporated into the British army. The procedure was directed by her Majesty's minister at Washington, Mr. Crampton, and the consuls in several important cities. The enemies of England did not fail to inform the Washington government as to what was going on. Protests were at once made diplomatically at London, and their result was seen in an order from the British Government forbidding the further execution of the scheme. It was asserted by Lord Clarendon, the Foreign Secretary, that no violation of the American laws had been contemplated or committed, and an interpretation of these laws was presented under which all that had been done was legal. Mr. Marcy, the Secretary of State, declined to adopt this interpretation and demanded the recall of Crampton. Upon the refusal of this demand, Crampton was notified that the President would have no further intercourse with him, and the notification was accompanied with his passport. At the same time, May, 1856, the exequaturs of three British consuls were revoked.

The dismissal of a minister is likely to be more thrilling in popular than in official circles. The whole progress of the affair was attended by violent declamation in the bellicose contingent of the press in both England and America. British excitement was enhanced by the simultaneous reports, persistently reiterated, that a ship under construction at New York was to

be a Russian privateer. Later the ministry
thought wise to reinforce the naval force at the
Bermudas, and this further nourished the prevailing war spirit. There was a good deal of
sentiment in England that the rather unsatisfactory meed of military glory acquired in the
now finished Crimean War should at once be
supplemented in a contest with the aggressive
Americans. No such feeling made any headway,
however, in the cabinet. Crampton's dismissal
was accepted as within the rights of the American Government. But he was knighted and
promoted. A new minister, Lord Napier, was
soon sent to replace him at Washington, and
to Napier's lot fell the duty of confirming a
satisfactory adjustment of all the outstanding
controversies between the two governments.

The war with Russia furnished the first situation since 1815 that might raise anew the
question of the right to impress sailors into
the British navy from American merchant vessels. There was some speculation as to the
possibility of a revival of the practice, and some
bristling discourse in the jingoistic American
press as to the dire consequences that would
follow. The generation that had elapsed since
the Napoleonic wars had brought changes,

however, which, without reference to the feeling of the Americans, rendered the idea of resort to the old method of recruiting by the British Government ridiculous. Nor did the power of Russia, as compared with that of her allied foes, suggest that Great Britain would be driven to desperate devices. Yet the British Government had never formally abandoned her claim to the right of search and impressment, and the memories and traditions of the way in which the right had been exercised in the old days undoubtedly sharpened the resentment in America at the operations for the enlistment of recruits for the army.

The time was now at hand for the termination of the long diplomatic difference between the two nations on the matter of the right of search. Complaints about the detention and search of American ships by British cruisers led to a renewed discussion of the procedure for the suppression of the slave-trade. This was in 1858, when the American interests were in the hands of President Buchanan and Secretary of State Cass, both men of long and intimate acquaintance with the diplomacy of this question. We have seen that the British contention in the matter had been reduced to

the claim of a right of visitation, as distinct
from the right of search, and that the American
view denied the validity of any such distinction.
Cass presented the American view in an elaborate note to Lord Napier on April 10, 1858, denying the "right of the cruisers of any other power
whatever, for any purpose whatever, to enter
their [United States] vessels by force in time of
peace." Lord Malmesbury, Foreign Secretary
in the cabinet of the Earl of Derby, which
interrupted the domination of Palmerston from
February, 1858, to June, 1859, declared in a
despatch to Napier that Great Britain recognized as sound "those principles of international
law which have been laid down by General
Cass in his note of the 10th of April." This
formal abandonment of the claim that had made
so much trouble between the two countries was
publicly avowed by Lord Malmesbury soon
afterward, who said: "We frankly confessed
that we have no legal claim to the right of visit
and of search which has hitherto been assumed."
So full and frank a confession of persistent error
afforded ample ground for the gratification felt
and proclaimed by President Buchanan. There
was involved in the British action no relaxation
of vigor in the suppression of the slave-trade,

no abandonment of the claim to the indefeasible allegiance of the subjects of the crown or of the right to force those subjects into the service of the navy. All that resulted from the new attitude of the British Government was the addition of that government's powerful support to the movement toward the freedom of the seas. So soon as the visitation of a vessel bearing the American flag ceased to be claimed as a right by Great Britain, the last great obstacle was removed that barred the most efficient co-operation for the suppression of the slave-trade. Within a few years the United States came to an agreement with Great Britain authorizing the cruisers of either nation to search a suspected slaver bearing the colors of the other. This arrangement had been diligently sought by the British Government for years, but the United States had held off so long as that was claimed as a right which they were willing to concede only as a conventional impairment of a right.

While the Central American situation and the other matters noticed above were dragging their troubled way to a settlement and engaging the chief interest of the two greater peoples of the English-speaking trio, the third member of the group passed through a series of interesting and somewhat critical experiences in both domestic and foreign affairs. The insurrectionary movements in Canada in the late thirties were followed, as we have seen, by the establishment of a new constitution in 1841, under which the two provinces were united into one. Party strife continued in the new system to centre about the same question that had been the core of controversy in the old, namely, how far the governor-general and his ministers should be subject to popular control. The problem was difficult. The administration of the colony must be subject to the control of the home ministry; how could it be subject at the same time to the direction of the majority in the legislative assembly? How could the connection with the British Empire be secure if Canadian policy must be determined by a majority that might follow a Papineau or a Mackenzie? So long as the Tory cabinet of Sir Robert Peel held sway at Westminster, with Lord Stanley at the Colonial Office, the old system continued to prevail in Canada. The popular opposition grew steadily stronger and more demonstrative as the fear of renewed violence wore away. The Whig cabinet that succeeded Peel in 1846 sent as governor-general to Canada the Earl of Elgin, son-in-law of Lord Durham. Elgin at once committed himself fully to the principle of ministerial responsibility. The first election after his accession to power resulted in a sweeping victory for the Reform or Liberal Party, and to the leader of this party's majority in the legislature Elgin intrusted the formation of a ministry. In this action the advance of democracy in Canada was definitely recognized, whatever the effect might be on the connection with the mother country. Within a few years responsible ministries were conducting the affairs of the other North American provinces also, without visible peril to the unity of the empire.

Lord Elgin's practical solution of the chief constitutional issue did not bring political calm in Canada. On the contrary, he had to deal with a particularly bitter revival of the race conflict that was latent in the party alignment. The strength of the Tories was in the English population of Upper Canada, while the Liberals had their largest membership among the French of the lower province. With the accession of the Liberals to power the long domination of the United Empire Loyalists ended, and the loss of place and privilege in the administration was attended by the ill feeling natural under the circumstances. Fear of approaching French ascendancy was widely proclaimed, and in a less degree actually felt. The disquiet was aggravated by one of the early acts of the Liberal legislature. This was a law giving compensation to loyal subjects in Lower Canada whose property had been destroyed in the military operations against the rebels in the late insurrection. A similar measure applying to Upper Canada had been passed by the Tories before their fall; their view in reference to the lower province was, however, that disaffection had been practically universal, and that compensation for losses would, therefore, be a premium on rebellion. The Liberals pushed their bill through in spite of the bitterest hostility, and Lord Elgin, with the assent of the home government, gave it his approval. One immediate result was that his Lordship was stoned by a mob, and the Parliament House was burned to the ground.

This riotous outbreak occurred in April, 1849, at Montreal. Other causes co-operated with the compensation bill to inflame the popular wrath. All Canada was suffering from a serious industrial depression. Montreal was the chief centre of business and the largest city of the colony. The distress among the people was peculiarly severe at this centre, and the material for a riotous assemblage was peculiarly plentiful. Montreal was, moreover, the chief seat of the English interest in Lower Canada, and the place in which the fear of French ascendancy was keenest. In 1849 a considerable group of influential men at Montreal were indicating a willingness to go even so far as separation from the British connection if that should prove the only means of escape from the evils that threatened or actually beset them. To understand the source of this extreme counsel it is necessary to look at the larger aspects of the free-trade reform and of Manchesterism in general so far as it affected the English-speaking world.

The protective system that Peel destroyed in 1846 was based primarily upon the purpose of benefit to the people of Great Britain, but it by no means disregarded the interests of the British subjects who lived in the colonies. Both customs and navigation laws included many and intricate provisions designed to give to the colonists advantages over all the world save the favored producers and merchants of the mother country. Canada, owing to its proximity to the United States and the identity of its chief products with those of the republic, required and possessed special preferences in the British tariff in order to maintain any satisfactory position in the competition with her more advanced and more populous neighbor. In 1843 the Peel government passed an act designed to aid agriculture in Canada, by giving to Canadian wheat and flour a much-reduced duty in Great Britain. The provisions of this act applied to all flour exported from Canada, regardless of the origin of the wheat. The effect of the law was soon manifest in a great development of the milling industry in the colony, with corresponding activity in commerce. American wheat was imported all along the border, turned into flour, and shipped from Montreal and Quebec to England, where the tariff barred direct importation from the United States.

The prosperity that followed the Canada Corn Act had just become generally manifest when in 1846 protection was abandoned and the ports of Great Britain were thrown open to wheat and flour from all the world. Every advantage enjoyed by colonial produce in the British mar-

ket was swept away by free trade. The result
in Canada was the prompt collapse of the industries that had been built up by the act of
1843. The short season of exaggerated prosperity was succeeded by a period of depression
and distress. Angry protests arose from the
capitalists and mercantile classes that they had
been ill treated by the home government. The
working class mobbed the governor, as we have
seen. In the destruction of their business the
Canadian Tories, who included the leading merchants of Montreal, found an aggravation of the
disregard for their feelings and interests that
was manifested in the "compensation for rebellion." Expressions of discontent began to take
on extreme form in the press and in the legislature. The cure for the existing and threatened evils that was most often proposed was
annexation to the United States.

During the year 1849 an agitation for annexation assumed proportions that attracted serious
attention. A manifesto issued at Montreal in
October, and signed by a large number of the
most substantial citizens, set forth the misfortunes and distress of Canada in temperate but
convincing terms, and argued that of all the
remedies suggested the only one that promised

results was "a friendly and peaceful separation
from British connection, and a union upon equitable terms with the great North American
confederacy of sovereign states." The revival
of protection in the United Kingdom could not
be depended on; a system of protection for
Canada might create manufactures but would
furnish no market for them; the same failure
would attend the suggested federation of the
American colonies or their independence. Unrestricted commercial intercourse with the great
population to the southward was indispensable
to the economic welfare of Canada, and this
could be secured only by incorporation into the
Union. Political advantages also would flow
freely from such a connection. With malicious
allusion to the late tension about Oregon and
the rising dispute over Central America, the
manifesto continued:

> Disagreement between the United States and her chief,
> if not only, rival among nations would make the soil
> of Canada the sanguinary arena for their disputes. . . .
> That such is the unenviable condition of our state of de-
> pendence upon Great Britain is known to the whole world;
> and how far it may conduce to keep prudent capitalists
> from making investments in the country, or wealthy set-
> tlers from selecting a foredoomed battlefield for the home
> of themselves and children, it needs no reasoning on our
> part to elucidate.

There was added a comparison of the dependence and subordination of the Canadians in the existing conditions with the proud equality they would enjoy as citizens of the United States. The honors and emoluments of the British Empire were denied them as colonials, while all the distinctions of the American Republic would be within their reach.

The movement of which this document was the pronunciamento was in Canada to a great extent an episode of provincial party politics. Support for it was drawn almost entirely from two sources, the Tories and the ultra-democratic element of the French Liberals. Such an alliance had no possibility of permanence or of effectiveness. What the one party had most at heart in the proposed union with the United States was wholly abhorrent to the other. The inner repugnance of the two elements was kept in abeyance at first, and for some months agitation through associations and public meetings was active and to the government disquieting. Though the annexationists invariably declared that the peaceful consent of Great Britain was an absolute prerequisite to the realization of their purpose, Lord Elgin, on the advice of his ministry, took pains to discourage the agitation, and excluded from the public service those who identified themselves with the movement. This was a severe blow to the Tory element of the discontented. The French element received a like setback through the strong and open condemnation of the agitation by the Catholic clergy. Good harvests and a revival of business served to alleviate the economic situation, and after some small successes in the elections in 1850 the organization and activity of the annexationists faded gradually away.

In neither Great Britain nor the United States did the movement in Canada attract much attention. Home politics in the great republic were just at the time in a state that left little room for public concern with matters beyond the border. Territorial extension had raised issues as to slavery that were threatening disruption of the Union. Under the circumstances a proposal of further extension could hardly be expected to enlist much enthusiasm. In some of the States contiguous to Canada the legislatures passed resolutions approving the idea of reuniting the long-severed members of the English-speaking race in North America. At Washington, however, there was no manifestation of feeling by either legislature or executive.

Indifference or positive hostility was indeed the attitude assumed toward even the projects of commercial reciprocity that were being urged upon the attention of the government by representatives of Canada.

At Westminster and in England at large the growth of the movement for annexation was followed naturally with rather closer interest. There was ample basis for the assertion of the Canadian agitators that their proposed remedy for colonial ills had its origin in Great Britain. Ultimate separation had long since been declared by distinguished Britons to be a natural incident of development in the colonies so soon as the union with the mother-land should become burdensome. On this principle, it was argued, the British Government's concern in the matter was limited to the question of separation. Assuming that the reasons for separation were sufficient, the determination as to what shall follow independence must be left to the colonists themselves. Annexation proper, therefore, was no matter for discussion with Great Britain.

During the process of transition from protection to free trade the debates of British politics had furnished an impressive addition to the list of great names sustaining the idea of even-

tual independence for the colonies.  All shades
of party opinion contributed to the list.  Protectionist Tories believed that the burden of
sustaining the colonies would be intolerable
now that the policy of exploiting them for the
benefit of the mother-land was given up.  The
Peelites and conservative Whigs contended that
free trade would prove the economic salvation
of both colonies and mother-land, and would
thus strengthen the bond uniting them, but admitted that if for any reason the interests of
either clearly should demand separation, there
would be no valid ground for opposing it.  Radicals proclaimed the democratic dogma of the
people's will and held that independence was
the right of the colonists whenever and for whatever reason they demanded it.  Disraeli, Peel,
Gladstone, and Lord John Russell all put on
record their conviction that British policy must
be shaped in contemplation of the gradual dissolution of the empire.  Cobden was, of course,
the high priest of this creed; but Cobden never
held the reins of governmental authority.  His
luminous expositions of the creed lacked the
immediate practical effect of such words as those
of Lord John Russell, prime minister, in 1850.
Concluding his speech in the Commons in which

he denounced the annexationists of Canada, he
said:

I anticipate indeed with others that some of the colonies may so grow in population and wealth that they
may say: "Our strength is sufficient to enable us to be
independent of England . . . the time is come when we
think we can, in amity and alliance with England, maintain our independence." I do not think that that time
is yet approaching. But let us make them as far as possible fit to govern themselves—let us give them, as far
as we can, the capacity of ruling their own affairs—let
them increase in wealth and population; and, whatever
may happen, we of this great empire shall have the con-
solation of saying that we have contributed to the happiness of the world.

This amiable and pacific pronouncement was
not relished by the Canadian authorities. It
involved a concession of the chief principle of
the annexationists and limited controversy with
them to the mere question of the proper time
for putting their project into effect. Lord
Elgin recorded a strong protest against the
prime minister's expressions, as seriously embar-
rassing to the colonial government. Russell
undoubtedly voiced, however, the prevailing
political philosophy of his day. The free-trade
movement in Great Britain presented a com-
bination of two clearly distinguishable elements, a refined and gentle idealism and a crude,

rough materialism. Its intellectual supporters considered unrestrained action in commerce and industry as but a further realization of the liberty that was natural to a rational being; free trade was a right of man like free speech and free worship; abolition of the protective tariff was a step toward the perfection of the individual and the race. In Cobden's expositions this philosophy was most skilfully blended with consideration of the practical needs of the British merchants and manufacturers. The latter, however, were little concerned about abstract liberty and the progress of the race. Free trade with them was a matter only of markets. Expansion of commerce, new consumers of commodities, enlargement of plants to the point of maximum production and profit—these summed up the advantages of free trade from the business man's point of view. To him colonists were but customers; to the idealists they were but men, with natural rights. That they were Englishmen and were determined by that fact from the beginning of the world to changeless political union with other Englishmen, was a conception that had no place in the thought of either element of the free-traders. The federation of the world and not imperial feder-

ation was the key-note of British liberalism
in 1850.

Lord John Russell's peremptory denial of
the claim that the time was ripe for Canadian
independence was preceded by legislation designed to remedy some of the ills that gave rise
to the claim.  In 1849 Parliament swept away
the last remnants of the old restrictive commercial system by repealing the famous Navigation Laws.  The operation of these laws
greatly aggravated the misfortunes that were
brought upon Canada by the abolition of
preferential duties in the mother country.  Colonial commerce with Great Britain was limited
to British ships, and freight rates were correspondingly high.  American competition, duly
favored by Congressional legislation, was able
thus to make sad inroads on various branches
of the trade with the home country.  Complaints from Canada became urgent at Westminster, and there was no room to doubt that
they were well founded.  The Whig cabinet,
therefore, resolved to complete the work that
Huskisson had begun twenty years before, and
the carrying trade between the colonies and the
United Kingdom was thrown open to the ships
of all the world.

The abandonment of the restrictive system generally by Great Britain left the North American colonies, and especially Canada, still in an uncomfortable plight. Free trade made their prosperity dependent on the commercial policy of the United States as fully as protection had kept it dependent on the policy of the United Kingdom. From the point of view of production the northern part of the United States and the British provinces were a unit; the output of their fields and forests was practically the same. From the point of view of markets the colonists were at a great disadvantage. In the United States population was much denser, and the facilities for transportation were vastly superior. The Canadians were not yet beyond the stage of canals, while on the other side of the border railways had attained a remarkable development. What was necessary to the prosperity of the Canadians was free access to the markets of the greater neighbor. But the Americans made no haste to remove the tariff barrier with which they had met the old policy of restriction. To the advances of the British Government looking to reciprocal free trade on the Canadian frontier they presented the old familiar question: What have you to offer in return? Fortunately a now long-standing dispute over the ancient subject of the fisheries enabled Westminster to make an answer that, after years of consideration, was accepted as sufficient.

We have seen that in 1818 the United States renounced the liberty of taking fish "within three marine miles of any of the coasts, bays, creeks, or harbors" of British America except certain clearly described portions of the shores of Newfoundland and Labrador. In the later thirties complaints began to be heard from Nova Scotia that the American fishermen were disregarding this agreement by plying their trade in the bays of that colony. Legislation was enacted to punish the intruders and ultimately British naval vessels were sent to patrol the coast. The Americans stoutly denied that they were intruding, and the seizure of their fishing-vessels gave rise to prolonged diplomatic proceedings.

It appeared that certain most valuable species of fish had, with the disregard of human conventions that is so characteristic of the lower species of animate things, manifested their presence in paying numbers much nearer land than the standard cod ever ventured. In pursuit of the profitable game the Americans were brought within what the British claimed were "bays," and as such were barred to the fishermen. A "bay," in the sense of the treaty, was, according to the contention of the British, any expanse of water designated by that name, so that an American fisherman was an intruder even twenty miles from land, if he was fishing in water that was called a bay. The Americans claimed that the term "bay" applied with certain qualifications only to an indentation of the coast-line of such size and shape that a ship, when entering it, must pass within three miles of the land. In its full development the British doctrine held that the "coasts" from which the Americans were excluded were defined by a broken line running from headland to headland, so that there was no right to fish within three miles of such a line. The American claim was that British jurisdiction extended no more than three miles from actual land, and that the geometrical lines from headland to headland included often large portions of the high seas that were free to all.

There was abundant material in this conflict for endless debate by the experts of the law of nations. Of most importance to the practical statesman was the simple fact that the Americans were as deeply interested to get admission to the inshore fishing as the Canadians were to get free access to the markets of the United States. The *quid pro quo* expected by the Washington government was at hand, and the bargain was formally struck in the Reciprocity Treaty of 1854, concluded by Lord Elgin and Secretary of State Marcy. By this agreement the Americans acquired again the liberty, renounced in 1818, of taking fish in the bays, harbors, and creeks of the British provinces (except Newfoundland), without restriction as to distance from the shore. The British colonists gained the coveted access to the American markets through the provision for the reciprocal admission duty-free of enumerated commodities that included the principal products of the soil, the mines, and the forests. Reciprocity was further applied through the admission of the Americans to the navigation of the Saint Lawrence River, and the admission of the Canadians to the navigation of Lake Michigan.

The effect of this treaty on the relations between the English-speaking peoples of the Western world was marked and salutary. Friction over the fisheries passed away. Trade increased by leaps and bounds. British America and the United States tended manifestly toward that economic solidarity which the geographic conditions seemed to make natural. In 1854, the last full year before the treaty went into effect, the total trade between the two peoples was about $35,000,000; in 1856, the first full year after the treaty went into effect, the total trade was $57,000,000. This increase signified more than a mere enhancement of mercantile profits. It meant the promotion of the neighborly spirit and feelings between neighbors. It meant that those people who lived on opposite banks of the Detroit or the Niagara River, or on opposite sides of a surveyor's line, should no longer meet with legal obstacles to the free intercourse that proximity invited. It meant a great multiplication of the social and financial ties across the frontier that are sure to be created by increasing trade. In any estimate of the influences that made for friendly and sympathetic relations among English-speaking peoples in 1860, the Reciprocity Treaty of 1854 must stand side by side with the diplomatic adjustments already described concerning Central America and the right of search.

The general international harmony and cordiality that pervaded the English-speaking world at the beginning of the sixties was destined to disappear for more than a decade through the conditions produced by the Civil War in the United States.  Before considering the unfortunate effects of that convulsion, let us note the salient features of the English-speaking world at this period, as compared with what the term had denoted at the date of the Treaty of Ghent, forty-six years in the past.

In numbers the United Kingdom no longer stood first.  With 10,000,000 more inhabitants than in 1814, its 29,000,000 fell short by 2,000,-000 of the population of the United States. British North America showed a sixfold increase to 3,000,000, of whom all but 500,000 were in Canada.  Among the scattered dependencies of Britain the vast spaces of Australia were beginning to fill up through the thirst for gold, and some half-million settlers were shaping the foundations of a new English-speaking commonwealth.  In none of these chief groups, however, was there such uniformity of English speech as to prophesy complete social and political concord.  The brogue of the Irish Celt, the barbarous dialect of the African slave, and the *patois* of the French *habitant* suggested grave problems of statecraft in Great Britain and America; while Australia at this date was so little developed as to make the ultimate triumph of English still problematical.

Economically Great Britain was in 1860, as she had been in 1814, the leading power of the world. In both trade and manufactures she stood easily first. Her mercantile marine and her navy still surpassed those of any other nation. Yet there was no such disparity between her and the American Republic as was so conspicuous half a century earlier. In the carrying trade of the world the United States was Britain's nearest rival. In manufactures British supremacy was confirmed by the transition from the domestic to the factory system, which was practically complete in England in 1860. This supremacy it was not yet in the power of the sparse population of the United States to contest. For one branch of textiles, however, and that a most important one, namely, cotton goods, the dependence of England on the Americans for raw materials was complete, as was foreseen by the leaders of the American secessionists.

Politically, also, British and American ideas and conditions were much less remote from each other than at the time of the Treaty of Ghent. Both peoples had been moving toward democracy. The Americans found little to obstruct their swift and steady advance. The British moved sluggishly on among the obstacles of century-old institutions and prejudices, and made certain, if less than rapid, progress. England could not show in 1860, as the United States could, manhood suffrage, one-year terms for important executive officers, or an elective judiciary. On the other hand, the Tory aristocracy that had controlled British policy in 1814 had passed from power forever. The Whig nobles were giving way, as a controlling political force, to the liberal and radical elements of their party, hot from Birmingham and Manchester. Though "the Dukes" continued to figure in the councils of the party, its vital energy centred elsewhere, and was nourished on projects touching the suffrage, the church, education, and landlords, that could be realized only after Palmerston and Russell had passed from the political stage and left Gladstone to transform the Whig into the Liberal Party. The ideas that were thus approaching their triumph in Great Britain were ideas that America claimed as peculiarly its own. They embodied the aspirations of the working classes and non-conformists in Great Britain and the great mass of the Irish. These were the classes best known and best understood in the United States. Politics that involved their point of view and their interests was intelligible to the Americans, while the politics of the aristocracy was unintelligible and hence repulsive. So far, therefore, as the character of British problems changed in the sense described, sympathetic and cordial relations were strengthened.

At just the period we are treating, moreover, the effects of the vast migration of English-speaking people that marked the middle of the century were fully manifest. In the fifteen years ending with 1860 4,700,000 emigrants left the United Kingdom, of whom something like three-fourths went to the United States. British America was the announced destination of a million of them; but the drift of the newcomers across the boundary from the provinces into the United States was continuous and on a large scale. The number who set out for the United States direct was 2,900,000.

Of the total from the United Kingdom Ireland furnished, of course, the very great majority. A million Irishmen emigrated to the

United States in the years 1847-52, and a quarter of a million went to British North America. The census of 1860 gave the number of natives of Ireland in the United States as 1,611,304; the number of English-born as 433,-494; of Scots as 108,518; of Welsh as 45,763. The Irish made an impression socially and politically that was even deeper than their excess in numbers would warrant. Their animosity toward the English made it imperative that a politician who needed their support should display in some form an anti-British feeling. The performances that were elicited by this requirement were at times disheartening to those who hoped for harmony; but the motive became in time so obvious and the act so perfunctory that "twisting the British lion's tail" lost all relation to serious thought. The tales of suffering in the famine and of heartless oppression by landlords doubtless roused much feeling as they circulated through America. On the other hand, the religion and various racial traits of the Irish tended to excite a hostility to them that counteracted much of their anti-British influence.

Among the elements that co-operated to determine the relations between the British and

the American branches of the English-speaking
people, contemporary literature was in 1860
of well-defined importance. By that date the
United States had fairly freed itself from the
reproach of utter unproductiveness in this field.
Only the most narrow and hidebound devotees
of expiring English Toryism still failed to find
a readable American book. Irving, Cooper,
and Poe had won distinct, if not wildly enthusiastic, recognition from the oracles of literary
taste in Britain. Prescott, Motley, and Emer-
son were receiving attention. Not a few other
writers were wresting from the cultivated classes
of the United Kingdom the hesitating admission that the American democracy might yet
mean something in the life of the spirit. The
harmonizing influence of this feeling had its
complement in the impression made by British
writers in America. The stars of the mid-
Victorian galaxy were glowing with meridian
splendor in 1860. Carlyle, Ruskin, Tennyson,
Browning, Dickens, Thackeray, and George
Eliot—to name but a few—were honored as
intensively, if not as extensively, in the United
States as in England. One of them, Charles
Dickens, had vogue and popularity far above
all the rest in the United States, and this de-

spite the lively resentment excited by the descriptions of Americans and their life in his *American Notes* and *Martin Chuzzlewit*. The explanation lay in the social stratum in which he almost exclusively found his inspiration. The life, aspirations, pleasures, and pains of the common people furnished all his material. These things the American masses could understand. From his stories they received a strong and lasting impression of plain people like themselves in England, living real and understandable lives down beneath the glorious but misty region where moved the lords and ladies, and the magnates of philosophy, art, religion, and politics, who were commonly the *dramatis personæ* of other writers of English fiction. When the Civil War in America brought tension of a most threatening sort between the two nations, the bonds of a common literature like this were of the highest service in averting rupture.

# CHAPTER V

## THE AMERICAN CIVIL WAR AND ITS EFFECTS

DESPITE repeated and notorious demonstrations of their error, idealists will doubtless continue in the future to maintain as in the past that an omelette can be made without breaking any eggs. Many of the good people who preached ardent abolitionism in the name of humanity were equally devoted to the propaganda of universal peace. The four years of desperate war that brought about the extinction of slavery in the United States presented awkward problems of comparative humanity, and vexed the spirits of all the English-speaking people in whom hostility to slavery had become strong. Ill feeling toward Great Britain was manifested in both the contending sections in America very early in the war. Ill feeling toward both sections was manifested quite as early in Great Britain. The balance among these various emotions at any particular time depended to a great extent upon the relation then seeming to exist between slavery and the objects of the war.

Fighting between South and North began on the clearly defined issue of political independence. Seven states, organized in a confederacy, claimed the rights and authority of a sovereign power, and expelled by force a body of troops that refused to recognize that claim. The reasoning by which the claim was sustained had as its basis the familiar democratic dogma that government is just only when it rests upon the will of the governed. There was no room to doubt, so the Southerners held, that the people of the seven States willed to be governed by the authorities of the Confederacy, and not by the organs of the government at Washington. Whether the manifestation of this will had been constitutional or revolutionary, might be debatable. In either case, however, the result was unassailable. No power on earth could justly dispute the authority of that government which the people of the South had set up. President Lincoln, when he sought to assert the power of a government which the people had repudiated, was but treading in the tyrant footsteps of George III in 1776.

The logical strength of this Southern argument could not be disputed. Nor could, on the other hand, the strength of the reasoning by

which it was controverted on behalf of the
North. The same dogma of popular sovereignty
served the one cause as the other. The will of
the people must prevail. But who were the
people? Since democracy became in the later
middle age a favorite dogma of radical philosophy, this question, Who are the people? has
been the source of half the political woes of
mankind. In 1861 Mr. Lincoln and the North
maintained that the people in whom sovereign
power inhered was the whole body of inhabitants of the United States; that no less aggregate possessed any of the attributes of sovereignty; that this body, expressing its will
through a constitutional majority, was supreme
as against any individual or group of individuals in the United States; and that refusal to
recognize such supremacy was simply treason.
The corroboration of this doctrine in the last
analysis was to be found in the dogma that
the United States was a nation, and the government at Washington was a national government. To the contemner of nationality and
its representatives was ascribed something of
the ineffable depravity that characterized him
who sins against the Holy Ghost.

When the beginning of the war in the United

States obliged the other English-speaking peoples to form some definite opinion as to the right and wrong of the disastrous situation, a judgment on the merits of the political and constitutional arguments was naturally very difficult. That a people possessed the right to determine what its government should be, had been a dogma of all English political philosophy since the Whig revolution of 1688. That a nation was entitled to independence and self-government, was, with certain qualifications adapted to the latitude of Ireland, an accepted maxim of British policy. But the application of these principles to the American situation was effectually barred by the very unanimity with which they were accepted by the contending sections. The South stood for sovereignty of the people (excluding negroes) and self-government for a nation, and stigmatized the North as a ruthless and bloodthirsty foreign invader. The North stood for sovereignty of the people (also excluding negroes) and self-government for a nation, and stigmatized the South as a lawless aggregate of rebels and traitors. Elaborate reasoning from history and law was adduced by both sides in support of their respective contentions; but this was even less successful abroad than at home in producing a consensus of opinion on the merits of the case. Political and legal theory was bankrupt in the presence of the fierce passions that dominated the American democracy, and recourse was had to other grounds when foreign judgment and sympathy were determined.

In Great Britain the South had from the outset the favor of the leading classes—the great newspapers and the most eminent men in politics and society. This was in some measure due to the almost universal acceptance of the ancient doctrine that a state of great area and population, under democratic political institutions, could not long endure. All thinkers of repute, for centuries in the past, had sustained this view, and it was ingrained in the intellectual apparatus of the age. France since 1789 was held to have confirmed the dogma. For three-quarters of a century the United States had thrived in defiance of this profound truth; but the secession of the South had at last justified the philosophers. As the South was but fulfilling the requirements of ineluctable fate, she was entitled to the respect and sympathy of mankind. There was current at the same time in the upper circles of

English society a conviction that the democracy of the South was much less pronounced and aggressive than that of the North—that the Southerner was more likely than the Northerner, on the average, to conform to the standards of the "gentleman," both in his social and his political ideas and actions. Of the two republics, therefore, into which the United States was henceforth to be divided, the Southern was to be the more amenable to British influence. Moreover, the policy of the South in respect to commerce was sure to be more in accord with the liberal views of Great Britain. Free trade was the manifest preference and the obvious interest of the South, while the recent recurrence of the North to protection, in the Morrill tariff of 1861, revealed a menace to the prosperity of British manufactures.

The Achilles heel of the Southern case before British opinion was slavery. Hostility to this institution was immovably fixed in the feelings of all classes of the people. Among the aristocracy, intellectual and social, there was appreciation of the hard problem of the Southern whites in dealing with the great mass of blacks on their hands, and there was corresponding toleration of the institution as a transitory solution; but there was no sympathy with the suggestion of permanent utility in slavery and of a revival of the African slave-trade, nor was there any approval of the idea that the maintenance of slavery was in itself a sufficient justification of secession by the South. Hence the unceasing vigilance of the most acute Southern leaders to avoid all discussion of the slavery question and to put the case of the South on the other grounds. This policy received much support from the Northern government itself in the early days of the war; for out of regard for sentiment in the non-seceded slave States President Lincoln's administration systematically kept abolitionist doctrine in the background, and based its appeal for support on the supremacy of the nation over the State. It is not at all surprising that foreign governments adopted at the outset the view that slavery was involved only incidentally in the quarrels of the sections.

One powerful element of public opinion in Great Britain adopted very early the view that slavery was the real cause of the war and that it was the duty of good people, therefore, to give their sympathy to the North. Such was the conviction reached by Cobden, Bright,

Forster, and Mill, under the influence of Sumner and other extreme antislavery doctrinaires. This judgment gained no great support in the higher classes of society, but, through the earnestness and eloquence of Bright and Cobden especially, won a vast body of adherents among the middle and lower classes, and thus secured for Charles Francis Adams, the American minister, a moral backing for which he was profoundly grateful. It was not till after the formal adoption of the policy of emancipation by President Lincoln, however, that the maximum influence of this particular element of British opinion was discernible.

At the outbreak of the war Lord Palmerston was prime minister, and Earl Russell was foreign secretary. When in April, 1861, large armies were called into the field by both the United States and the Confederacy, privateers were commissioned by the South, and a blockade of the Southern ports was proclaimed by President Lincoln, it was clearly time for the British Government to recognize the situation. Commercial relations with both sections were vast and intricate, and with privateering in full sway on one side and blockade proclaimed on the other, trouble for British merchants and mariners was plainly in sight. What to do seems not to have caused any serious anxiety to the cabinet. The United States had followed the long-foreseen course of nature and had fallen in pieces. The pieces were at war with each other, and it was incumbent on the British Government to assume promptly the attitude and the duties of a neutral. Accordingly, on May 13, the Queen's proclamation of neutrality was issued. In this the proceedings in the United States were referred to as hostilities "between the government of the United States and certain states styling themselves the Confederate States of America," and all subjects of the Queen were notified that acts in violation of neutrality would bring heavy penalties upon the offender.

Here began an Iliad of woes for the English-speaking peoples. By this proclamation the British Government recognized the Confederacy as a belligerent, with the rights and responsibilities ascribed to a power engaged in international war. To the North, which considered the Confederates as mere riotous assemblages of rebels and traitors, the attitude of the British Government appeared to be a manifestation of open hostility. It gave to the insurgents a dignity which they had not deserved, and encouraged them beyond measure. Not only in the press and in popular speech, where the law and practices of war were not understood in their details, but also in the despatches of Secretary Seward and other diplomatic proceedings, resentment against Great Britain was open and bitter. It happened that the offending proclamation was promulgated on the very day that the new minister from Washington, Charles Francis Adams, reached London, and before he had entered upon his duties. This, to the agitated North, proved that the British Government hastened its action designedly, to avoid listening to the arguments against it, and to make clear beyond controversy a sympathy with the Confederacy. The distrust and hatred engendered by this proclamation of neutrality continued to determine for a generation the feeling of a great body of influential Americans toward the ruling classes of Great Britain.

The alienation of the North from the British was not accompanied by any marked growth of friendliness between the British and the South. The Palmerston cabinet devoted itself to the maintenance of the most rigid impartiality between the two contending sections of the

Americans. Earl Russell consistently refused official intercourse with the commissioners sent by the Confederate Government to England, and the instructions as to enforcement of neutrality by the local and colonial officials of the empire showed no special favor whatever for either of the belligerents. The South was indeed gratified by the proclamation of neutrality; but its chief hope of early success in establishing independence rested on the expectation of a more complete recognition by Great Britain—a recognition through the reception of its diplomatic representatives in their official character. The refusal of such reception in the spring and summer of 1861 caused mutterings and disquiet among the more ardent Southerners, with subdued curses of the abolitionism that was believed to poison the sources of British policy. After the triumph of the Confederates at Bull Run in July, hope took on a brighter hue. All the reports from England teemed with evidence of unofficial sympathy with the South and confidence in its success. The impending cotton famine, which was expected to force the government to action by the ruin of Lancashire, was already beginning to make itself felt. To be quite ready for the change of attitude that seemed near at hand, the Confederate Government designated a minister for Great Britain and one for France, and despatched the two to their posts. Before they reached their destinations they contributed much to the cause they represented, but involuntarily and in a manner that was in no wise contemplated in their instructions. After their destinations were reached, their contributions to the cause of the Confederacy were negligible.

On November 8, 1861, the two ministers, Mason and Slidell, were forcibly taken from the British mail-steamer *Trent* by Captain Wilkes, of the United States man-of-war *San Jacinto*. The captives were taken to the United States and by order of the government put in confinement as prisoners of war. Wilkes's action was entirely of his own initiative. Though it was a matter of general knowledge that the two ministers were on their way to Europe, and though there was a passionate desire in the North to prevent them from getting there, no orders for their capture had been issued. The news of their seizure was the signal for a rapturous outburst of rejoicing in the North. Wilkes was officially thanked by the Secretary of the Navy and by the House of Representatives; his praises were voiced in countless unofficial ways by countless unofficial persons. In the swelling chorus of popular approval the dominant note was the efficient patriotism of the commander in seizing the traitors and thwarting their plans. Here and there was clearly audible, however, another note—the shrill, wild cry of vengeful joy that Wilkes, in doing his duty, had flouted the flag of Great Britain. Governor Andrew, of Massachusetts, at a banquet given in honor of Wilkes, proclaimed it the crowning satisfaction of the whole affair that the commander "fired his shot across the bows of the ship that bore the British lion at its head." It is hardly doubtful that the rejoicing at the North owed half its ecstasy to the fact that the *Trent* was a British vessel.

There were a few cool heads in the North that believed Wilkes's action unwise and unjustifiable by the law of nations. By these men the course of Great Britain was awaited with serious foreboding. Their anxiety was not diminished by the news that reached America on December 12 of the overwhelming storm of rage and warlike fervor that swept over England when the proceeding of Wilkes became known. Philosophical observers were rare in those days, but the situation must have appealed with strange bewilderment to such as there were. Americans were splitting their throats with joyous approval of a harsh, crude exercise of the right of visitation and search; Englishmen were girding up their loins for war in defence of the rights of neutrals. The men of 1812—Castlereagh, Canning, Madison, John Quincy Adams—would have been in sad straits to adjust themselves to this extraordinary reversal of national rôles. What explained it lay for the most part beneath the surface. The Americans exulted not more over the capture of two conspicuous domestic foes than over the incidental flouting of the British flag, finding in this latter a fitting retaliation for the hostile haste in recognizing the Confederacy as a belligerent. The British, for their part, took high ground on the rights of the neutral flag less because those rights were apparently assailed than because the apparent assailant was the Yankees; for there was persistently current in England a suspicion that the Lincoln administration intended to make trouble with her for the sake of improving its position in home politics.

The course adopted by the Palmerston cabinet left no room for diplomatic subtleties or for political finesse in the adjustment of the *Trent* affair. Three days after the report of the affair was received, a despatch was sent to Lord Lyons at Washington instructing him to demand the surrender of Slidell and Mason, and a suitable apology for the affront to the British flag. In case the demand should not be complied with in seven days, the minister was directed to close the legation and leave Washington. The transmission of these instructions was accompanied by open and strenuous preparations for war. Exportation of military stores was forbidden; arsenals and dockyards hummed with access of industry; great quantities of arms and ammunition were hastily shipped to the North American provinces; most impressive of all, several thousands of troops, including a regiment of the Guards, embarked for the same destination.

Confronting such a situation, the Lincoln administration had no choice of policy. To think of conquering the Confederates after Great Britain should become their ally, was beyond the bounds of sanity. Accordingly, the captive envoys were put at the disposal of Lord Lyons, and were duly conveyed by a British war-ship back to the West Indies, whence they resumed their journey in triumph to England.

In announcing compliance with the British demand, Secretary Seward did what was possible
to save the face of the Americans. He wrote
with one eye on the British fleet and the other
on the Northern people. Such strabismic adjustment of the gaze does not conduce to clarity
of vision, and Seward's paper elicited scant applause from the experts of international law.
His contention was that Wilkes was wholly justified in stopping the *Trent* and searching her
for the Confederate envoys, but committed an
error when, having found them, he omitted to
bring the ship into port as a prize and secure a
judicial condemnation of her for violating the
laws of war by carrying contraband persons and
despatches. The Northern people were assured, that is, that Wilkes must be disavowed
not because he insulted the British flag, but
because he did not in addition capture it. Earl
Russell's reply to this despatch naturally controverted this view of the law of the case, and
argued elaborately that there was no warrant
in the law of nations for the interruption of the
*Trent's bona fide* course from one neutral port
to another. He reinforced his argument by
the discomforting suggestion that the principle
by which the act of Wilkes was justified would

equally justify the search at any time, by either a Confederate or a Federal cruiser, of the Dover-Calais packet, and its conveyance to America if agents or despatches of the enemy should be found aboard. How utterly at sea the experts were in regard to the law applicable to this case, and how little the technical law had to do with the practical policy adopted, appears in the fact that the law officers of the crown, at almost the exact moment when Wilkes threw his shell across the bows of the *Trent*, gave their opinion that the course which he, all unknown to them, was actually pursuing was strictly conformed to the precedents of British practice.[1] Later, these same legal authorities modified their opinion and solemnly declared that the law required that the offending neutral ship on which contraband persons or despatches were found must be taken to the captor's port and passed upon by a prize court—the precise ground that Seward took in his despatch and that Russell controverted in his reply.

The surrender of Mason and Slidell was so clearly a case of hard necessity that Northern opposition to it was scanty. The hatred of

[1] C. F. Adams, *The Trent Affair*, in Proceedings of the Massachusetts Historical Society, XLV.

Britain that it engendered was, however, general in prevalence and malignant in expression. Everywhere the thought was current: Great Britain has taken advantage of our weakness to browbeat and humiliate us. We will settle our domestic troubles and bide our time for revenge. Hamilcar's classic procedure recurred to many minds; and an inspection of London clubs to-day would probably reveal more than one elderly American dozing the pleasant hours away in happy forgetfulness of a Hannibalic obligation of enmity to Albion, assumed under paternal direction at the dim Christmastide of 1861.

The smart of defeat was not diminished by the taunts and jibes that issued in a broad, full stream from the British, Canadian, and Confederate press. "Swagger and ferocity, built on a foundation of vulgarity and cowardice," was sweetly declared by the London *Times* to be the compendium of Captain Wilkes's characteristic qualities, and he was, it said, "an ideal Yankee." Secretary Seward was described in hardly more complimentary terms, and was credited with a set purpose to pick trouble with Great Britain. The secretary's reputation as a reckless chauvinist and an undisguised Anglophobe seems indeed to have had much influence in official as well as in popular circles, and to have played a considerable part in determining the ministry to a hard, brusque demand for reparation. Earl Russell was not naturally disposed to harshness, and his assumption of so uncompromising an attitude was apparently due to a purpose not to give Seward any chance to win popular applause.

As to the Southerners, some pains were taken to show them that British policy was not chosen with any least reference to their interests. The arrival of Mason and Slidell in England was ostentatiously ignored by the cabinet, and *The Times* served semi-official notice on them in advance that they were not to assume the airs or expect the halo of martyrs. They could well afford, however, to submit with cheerfulness to such snubbing; for they were cordially received in aristocratic society, and they perceived on every side the currents of public opinion setting strongly in favor of the Confederate cause. Throughout the year 1862 the utter failure of the North to gain any decisive advantage in the field confirmed the conviction that the South could not be conquered, and that the vast sacrifice of blood and treasure in the attempt was inhuman and should be stopped. In Lancashire poverty and distress among the cotton-workers became extreme, and added a powerful practical argument in favor of steps toward opening the ports of the South. Yet the ministry persisted in its refusal to receive Mason or to adopt the projects of mediation and intervention that were from time to time seriously considered. Its rigidly correct attitude as a neutral in this respect resulted in a steadily growing hatred on the part of the South, which abandoned in the autumn of 1863 all efforts at diplomatic intercourse.

The alienation of the South from the British Government was not accompanied by any access of friendly feeling on the part of the North. On the contrary, the angry passions kindled by the proclamation of neutrality and the *Trent* affair found ever fresh fuel to maintain the flame. During 1862 blockade-running between the Confederacy and the British ports of the Bermudas and the Bahamas assumed large and spectacular proportions, and the cruisers *Florida* and *Alabama* began their destructive raids on the maritime commerce of the North. Popular sentiment, little versed in the niceties of neutral obligations, instinctively laid at Britain's door the responsibility for all the loss and humiliation due to these proceedings. Nor did the Lincoln government fail to make an adequate and proper appeal to the British ministry for a more rigorous and efficient enforcement of its own laws touching such matters. Charles Francis Adams had a task more delicate and exacting than that of either his father or his grandfather at the court of Saint James's, and the perfect success with which he performed it has been recognized in full by his adversaries. He brought Earl Russell to realize that the *Alabama* should not be permitted to sail from Liverpool, though the earl's order to detain her arrived too late to serve its purpose. A year later, when a far more serious menace to the Northern cause was prepared by the clever Confederate agents in England, and two great ironclads were nearing completion by the same firm that built the *Alabama*, Adams went to the verge of a hostile rupture before he persuaded Russell to seize the vessels. The detention of the ironclads was a sickening blow to the hopes of the South. In the North it caused great elation, but it served at the same time to evoke the truculent vow that when the Union should have been made secure the failure of the British to detain the *Alabama* also should be put before them for explanation and settlement.

Such was the disturbing spirit with which the North approached its triumph in 1865. The friendship and harmony that were conspicuous among English-speaking peoples in 1860 had been supplanted by as unprepossessing an aggregate of evil emotions as the inferno of a four years' desperate war could be expected to produce. The victorious people, with an army of a million men, a navy of five hundred ships, a crushed and helpless rival at its feet, looked round to see if any scores remained to be settled. Against every other branch of the English-speaking race the flushed and angry conqueror believed that it had a grievance to present. The West Indian colonists had sustained and thrived by the blockade-runners, through whom the Confederacy had preserved its life long after the end was assured. The Canadians and their associates of the Maritime Provinces had given refuge to Confederate agents who had organized expeditions of rapine and murder across the Northern boundary. In the African and Asiatic colonies of England the *Alabama* and other cruisers had received indispensable aid in their

piratical enterprises. Even from remote Australia came eventually reports that the last of
the Confederate cruisers, the *Shenandoah*, had
been enabled by illegitimate privileges allowed to
it at Melbourne to destroy the American whal-
ing fleet in the Arctic seas. Every item in this
account—and by no means all the items familiar
in 1865 have been catalogued here—was charged
with bitterness, hatred, and a longing for revenge. Nor were these emotions less conspicuous in the conquered South than in the victorious North. Recognition by Great Britain for
the sake of cotton had been the rock bottom on
which Confederate hopes were built. Refusal of
this recognition left a feeling that Great Britain
was wholly responsible for the ensuing catas-
trophe, and not a few voices were heard from
the ruins of the South declaring that, if a settlement of old scores with that power should be
undertaken, Lee's veterans would not be slow
to join Grant's in the enterprise.

The vindictive feeling in the United States
declined in aggressiveness as Napoleon's insolent
challenge across the Rio Grande engaged attention, and as the problems of reconstructing the
South became more and more absorbing. Yet
governmental action, legislative, diplomatic, and

administrative, as well as movements of the
popular spirit, continued to reveal the working
of the latent hostility.  The happy relations
built up by Lord Elgin between the United States
and Canada suffered hopeless damage.  Even
the ancient and indurated Rush-Bagot arrangement came into imminent peril of extinction.
During 1864 Confederates from Canada captured steamers on Lake Erie and also made a
raid on a town in Vermont.  After these affairs
Secretary Seward gave notice that the Rush-
Bagot arrangement would be disregarded after
six months.  In March of 1865, however, he
withdrew this notice of abrogation, and announced that the United States would continue
to observe the terms of the arrangement.

The Reciprocity Treaty of 1854 in respect to
Canadian trade met with a less kindly fate.
Complaints of unfairness in the working of the
treaty became common in the United States
only a few years after it went into operation.
These gained in force and volume as the beginnings of tariff protection to manufacturers
appeared in Canada.  The revival of protectionism in the United States in connection with
the war strengthened the foes of the treaty, but
the impulse that was decisive of its fate was

apparently due to the anti-British feeling engendered by the incidents of the war.  Congress
directed by act of January 18, 1865, that the
requisite one year's notice of abrogation be
given, and accordingly the provisions went out
of effect in 1866.  By this action the unsatisfactory conditions as to the inshore fisheries revived, and a period of friction over this troublesome matter was prepared.

Still more directly and obviously the outcome
of the changed feeling toward Great Britain
was the support given to the earnest but rather
absurd undertakings of the Fenians.  Among
the millions of Irishmen in the United States
hatred of all things British was practically
universal.  Any project, however chimerical,
for breaking the power of the "Saxon" was sure
of wide sympathy and support from Irish-
Americans.  In the armies that fought the war
of secession the Irish were conspicuous in both
numbers and achievement.  When the armies
were disbanded many of these veterans were
easily induced to join the Fenian movement—
an enterprise directed with rather ostentatious
secrecy to the establishment of an independent
republic in Ireland.  It would not seem likely,
*a priori*, that the first overt step toward this

end should be an invasion of Canada by an
Irish army. Yet such was in fact what occurred.
Considerable bodies of Fenians, with some rudimentary organization and equipment as a military force, assembled along the northern frontier of the United States, and in the summer
of 1866 crossed into Canada at various points.
They were promptly chased back across the border by the Canadians, and were then gathered
up and sent to their homes by the authorities
of the United States. It was not creditable to
the government at Washington that such an
attack on a neighbor from its territory was not
prevented. In explanation it could only be
said that the proceeding was so inherently
fatuous as never to have warranted an expectation that it would be actually undertaken.
Beyond this, however, was the undoubted fact
that the minor officials from whom the earliest
reports of impending trouble should have come
had very little disposition to be vigilant in
warding off trouble from Great Britain. The
conviction that the British Government had
not overstrained its vigilance in connection
with the *Alabama* was thus producing results.

Evidence that the grievance against Great
Britain was actively operating on the American

mind at the time when the Fenian disturbance was at its height is to be seen in the action of the House of Representatives in relation to the neutrality laws. In the summer of 1866 the House passed by a unanimous vote a bill to repeal the prohibition, in those laws, of fitting out ships for belligerents. The bearing of this is clearer when connected with the suggestion made in debate that the "Republic of Ireland" be recognized as a belligerent. When, a year or two later, there was war between Great Britain and Abyssinia, an Anglophobe senator introduced and sustained with great vigor a resolution recognizing King Theodore as a belligerent, and authorizing him to fit out privateers in the ports of the United States.

In Ireland and England the Fenians manifested their existence through a long series of plots and ineffective lawlessness. Very many of those who were most active in these operations had duly equipped themselves with the rights of American citizenship. At no time after the first weeks of 1866 were the British authorities in the least danger from the Fenians. The government had the situation well in hand, and the arrests of offenders went on without ceasing. Naturally, loud appeals for help came in an endless stream from the unfortunate American citizens to Mr. Adams in the legation at London. The minister had little taste for the special kind of duty that this situation imposed. His chief function had become, so he wrote privately to Seward, to rescue Irishmen from punishment which in most cases they richly deserved. There was often at issue, however, in these cases a principle that was well worthy of most serious diplomatic attention. Ever since the great immigration from Europe began in the forties, the American Government had been under pressure to assert for its naturalized citizens the same rights in the land of their birth that were granted to native-born American citizens. Grave and well-founded objections to this claim were raised by foreign governments, who denied the right of expatriation. There was a very natural disposition in Great Britain, for example, to manifest special rigor in the case of an Irishman who used an easily acquired American citizenship as a cover for promoting in Ireland the cause of the Fenians. In the United States every such instance evoked a passionate Celtic clamor, whose influence appeared at every session of Congress and in every electoral campaign. To reflecting and well-bal-

anced Americans the qualifications with which
the claims of the naturalized citizens were to
be taken were obvious; yet the incessant denunciation of Great Britain by the Irish and
their friends inevitably strengthened the current of ill feeling that derived its portentous
volume from other sources.

While American feeling and policy were taking the forms that have been noticed, what were
the effects in Great Britain of the triumph of the
North?  Sir George Cornewall Lewis, a member of the Palmerston cabinet, recorded in the
midst of the tumult the opinion that the civil
war in the United States was a phenomenon of
world-wide significance, not a mere local fray.
The soundness of the judgment has been continuously confirmed as the decades have passed
along, but it was discernible very early in the
effect of the conflict on the trend of British home
politics.  The division of sympathy in England
as between the two contending sections followed
pretty closely the cleavage between the social
classes whose antagonism was crossing and con-
fusing the old party alignment.  The Duke of
Argyll, sustaining the North, and Laird and
Roebuck, sustaining the South, were indeed
examples of deviation that served to emphasize

the rule; but Bright and Cobden, leading the lower middle and working classes, with Gladstone and Palmerston speaking for the upper middle class and the titled aristocracy, were the typical exponents of the respective sympathies. When the Emancipation Proclamation seemed to announce the extinction of slavery as the purpose of the North, a perceptible gain in favor for that section followed, and those humanitarians who had committed themselves to the South were called upon to revise or explain their position.  Their task was no harder than that of the Quaker, John Bright, who in 1854 was full of scorn for the idea that there could be any connection between the slaughter of thousands and the cause of freedom, but ten years later found the slaughter of hundreds of thousands abundantly justified by the liberation of the blacks.[1]

As a matter of fact, a fundamental influence in fixing the sympathies of Britons was the more or less unconscious perception of a relation between the American problem and their own.  The liberalizing and democratizing spirit was steadily disintegrating both the old political parties.  Those who welcomed the work of

[1] Trevelyan, *Life of John Bright*, 226, 318.

this spirit longed for the preservation intact of the American Union as the model of a great and prosperous democracy. Those who dreaded the approach of democracy were quick to see in the American war a proof of its weakness and futility.

When, in the course of 1864, the strangling and crushing of the Confederacy by the terrific power of the North became pretty clearly a matter of time alone, Southern sympathy in England ceased to manifest itself. Politicians and scholars who had portrayed with eloquence and learning the inherent vices of democracy and the impossibility of its application in the government of large populations, abandoned in silence the field of political theory and prophecy. The complete triumph of the North in the spring of 1865 was attended by a great impetus to the radical propaganda of Bright and his Manchester followers. The Whig and Tory aristocracy were badly discredited, and with the death of Lord Palmerston lost their ancient control over the government. For three years, indeed, Earl Russell and the Earl of Derby maintained the nominal succession of the old order, but Gladstone and Disraeli were the real representatives of the actual controlling power, which lay in a social stratum below that of Russell and Derby. This new power received its formal recognition in the British system through the Reform Bill of 1867, which gave a wide extension to the suffrage. It is hardly too much to say that the Reform Bill of 1867 was a direct product of the Northern triumph in the American war. Extension of the franchise was forced upon ministerial attention by Bright and the radicals, was undertaken in vain by Gladstone and the Russell government, and was actually enacted by the Derby cabinet, with the cynical Disraeli in the lead. This peculiar record of its genesis shows the wide basis of public opinion on which it was reared, and in this shows the far-reaching influence of the American situation.

While the end of the war brought little abatement of the ill feeling in the United States toward the British, there was in England a somewhat pronounced reaction toward amicable sentiments even among those classes whose distress at the success of republican ideas was deepest and most sincere. The tragedy of Lincoln's death had much to do with this movement. The most stolid Tory could not resist the softening effect of that most pathetic sequence—the divinely humane inaugural of

March 4, the triumph at Appomattox of April 9, and the assassin's bullet of April 14. No class of British society denied to Abraham Lincoln a high place among the heroes of the English-speaking race, and none could evade the truth, proclaimed by the whole story of his life, that he was the purest possible product, as well as the successful leader, of the American democracy.

For the seven full years following the end of the war in the United States, diplomacy found engrossing labor in the task of restoring the concord that was so rudely shattered in 1861. Domestic problems of highest significance diverted popular attention in large measure from a dangerous international situation. Reconstruction in the United States, federation in Canada and her British neighbors, electoral reform and Irish disestablishment in the United Kingdom—these insured to the foreign offices much-needed time for their slow pacific processes. The ministers labored always in the consciousness of impending peril. It was the heroic age of the Hohenzollern monarchy, and German unity was taking shape at Bismarck's bidding out of the ruin of Prussia's neighbors. Denmark was partitioned in 1864; Austria, Hanover, and some of the smaller German fry were crushed two years later; all the world knew that war with France was coming next. How far the unifying energy of the new Germany would extend, was uncertain. That Great Britain might become involved in war, if Holland or Belgium should be proclaimed indispensable to the territorial integrity of the German or the French nation, was obvious to all. When Denmark was attacked in 1864 it had not been perfectly easy to keep Great Britain out of the fray, though the non-interference policy had prevailed. The difficulty of such a policy in connection with aggression upon the Low Countries would be insuperable. And what was clear to all who stopped to think at all on the subject was, that the day when Great Britain declared war would witness the adoption by the United States of a policy as to neutrality that would encourage the use of American shipyards and ports by the enemies of Britain for the destruction of her commerce. Even in lack of formal announcement of such a policy *Floridas* and *Alabamas* would be sure to escape the drowsy vigilance of the authorities, and to pursue their devastating careers under guarantee of the same *non possumus* with which Earl Russell had met the reclamations of Secretary Seward.

From the July day in 1862 when the "No. 290" passed out of the Mersey on her "trial trip," to become the redoubtable *Alabama*, responsibility for the damage done by her to American commerce was formally and systematically charged upon the British Government by Seward and Adams. The long lists of vessels captured and destroyed that came in to the State Department at Washington were duly submitted to Earl Russell, with intimations that indemnity would be expected from Great Britain. Because the operations of the *Alabama* were so far-reaching and so successful, they assumed very great prominence in diplomatic as in popular discussions, and by the end of the war the term "*Alabama* claims" was commonly used to designate the whole mass of complaints against the British Government for the favor that it was alleged to have shown to the Confederacy in violation of its profession of neutrality. The use of the term in this broad sense reflected and stimulated a feeling in America that British delinquency was of a kind that could not be atoned for by mere financial compensation for the losses caused by the Confederate cruisers.　The existence of this feeling and the bitterness with which it was resented in England give a clue to some of the most serious complications of ensuing years.

While war was flagrant, claims based on acts of the *Alabama* were presented by Secretary Seward, and rejected by Earl Russell, with monotonous frequency.　A rather peevish request of Russell that the annoying procedure be abandoned was followed by some curtailment of the arguments that accompanied the claims, but not of the lists of losses.　In 1865, when the Confederacy was in ruins and the last cruiser had abandoned her career of destruction, the two governments girded themselves for the diplomatic contest that was now possible without the distractions of hostilities. The complete case for the United States combined the Queen's proclamation of neutrality with the government's derelictions of duty in respect to the cruisers as a comprehensive manifestation of partiality to the Confederacy, and a wrong to the American nation.　The proclamation of neutrality, Adams argued, was premature and unfriendly.　In recognizing the insurgents as belligerents on the ocean before they had a single vessel afloat, her Majesty's

government had acted in a manner that was
without precedent in the practice of nations.
This action in its essence created an ocean belligerent instead of recognizing one that was
already self-created. Thereafter the belligerent character on the ocean was maintained
exclusively by vessels built, equipped, and
manned in British ports, in spite of protests by
the United States and demands that such viola-
tions of neutrality be prevented. Freely con-
ceding the desire of her Majesty's government
to maintain a real neutrality, Adams declared
that all efforts to that end had proved ineffec-
tual, first because the laws were inadequate,
and second because the government did not
secure such change in the laws as would have
healed the defects. In consequence of this
failure of real neutrality, hundreds of American
ships, with millions of dollars' worth of cargo,
had been destroyed, and the commercial marine
of the United States had been transferred to
the protection of the British flag, insuring thus
to the British people an unjust advantage from
the wrong committed against a friendly nation.
For such manifest injuries, due to the defects
in the British law and the failure of the government to remedy them, the United States was

entitled in reason and justice to reparation and indemnity.

Earl Russell's response to these representations was in substance as follows. When her Majesty's Government, on May 13, 1861, recognized the Confederacy as a belligerent power, it was in fact a belligerent, acknowledged to be such by official act of the United States Government. The fact of belligerency was clear from the great population and territory controlled by the Confederacy, its complete governmental organization, its large armies and numerous fortresses, its undeniable exercise *de facto* of all forms of sovereign authority, including the issue of letters of marque. The recognition of belligerency by the United States was equally clear from the blockade of the Confederate coast officially announced by President Lincoln before the 13th of May; and this view had been sustained by the Supreme Court of the United States. The British Government, if it did not recognize the Confederates as belligerents, would have been obliged to treat them as outlaws and pirates, and this the government was unwilling to do in the case of so large, well-organized, and valiant a population. The demands of British merchants and ship captains, moreover, for directions as to their rights and duties in the circumstances, made the government's prompt action necessary. As to later questions, Lord Russell stoutly contended that his government had enforced with fairness and impartiality the neutrality which was proclaimed. The Foreign Enlistment Act authorized the seizure of a ship that was proved to be armed and equipped, wholly or in part, in British jurisdiction, for the purpose of naval service for a power at war with a power friendly to her Majesty. The proof required by the act as preliminary to seizure was very difficult to obtain. Of nineteen vessels complained of by Mr. Adams, however, only five actually hoisted the Confederate ensign, and of these one never got into actual service, and another was seized but released after trial, for lack of sufficient evidence as to her warlike character. Under such circumstances, Lord Russell argued, it was idle to accuse the government of inefficiency in the performance of its duties under the law.

As to the ships that escaped the vigilance of the authorities, his Lordship held the methods employed by the Confederate agents to have been so skilfully adapted to their purpose that

only the arbitrary and inquisitorial procedure
of despotic governments could have thwàrted
them.  To build a ship is the undoubted right
of every Englishman.  To set sail with a party
for a foreign land, is equally the right of all.
To ship cannon and munitions of war to foreign destinations is also a right of Britons.
When the ship and the party and the cannon and
munitions, after leaving British waters, come
together and coalesce into a Confederate cruiser,
the British Government may feel deceived and
flouted, but it cannot be held responsible for inefficiency.  On this principle every case alleged
against Great Britain by the United States
failed absolutely except that of the *Alabama*.
In this instance evidence as to her true character was pronounced by the law officers of the
crown sufficient to justify her seizure, and
orders to hold her reached Liverpool in the
afternoon of the day on which she passed in
the morning out to sea.  Lord Russell was
greatly angered at this peculiar coincidence,
and there was no room to doubt the sincerity
of his assurance of regret to the American minister.  Yet he was wholly justified in arguing
that the failure of duty by subordinates of the
administration was no sufficient basis for the

sweeping charge of bad faith and hostile animus against the British Government.

Lord Russell's discussion in 1865 with Mr. Adams culminated in a rather brusque rejection of the proposal, submitted in a more or less tentative way by the American some two years earlier, looking to arbitration. The only questions to be submitted to an arbiter, Russell said, would be, first, whether the British Government had acted "with due diligence, or, in other words, in good faith and honesty," in maintaining neutrality; second, whether the law officers of the crown properly understood the Foreign Enlistment Act when they gave their opinions as to its application to the cases of the *Alabama* and other cruisers. To put either of these questions to the representative of a foreign government, would be incompatible, he held, with regard for the dignity and character of the British crown and the British nation. "Her Majesty's government must, therefore, decline either to make reparation and compensation for the captures made by the *Alabama*, or to refer the question to any foreign state."

The most that Lord Russell saw his way to do in the existing situation was to set up a joint commission to pass upon all claims arising on either side out of the Civil War, provided, as he explained with great care, that the claims concerned in the exploits of the cruisers should be excluded. This proposition was declined by Seward with no less directness than that which Russell displayed in declining arbitration.

It was soon evident that the attitude assumed by Earl Russell failed to win the support of important elements of British public opinion. The maritime commercial interest perceived with ever-increasing vividness the peril to English trade that was involved in any relaxation of neutral duties. Party leaders were embarrassed by the strained relations with the United States. Respect for the American Republic was general, and admiration even was found in many circles where only contempt had appeared before Appomattox. With a realizing sense of the losses inflicted by the *Alabama,* and the knowledge that orders to detain her were actually issued by the government, many voices were heard in high quarters declaring that there was ground for the complaints of the Americans, and that the best British policy would be to reach a settlement as speedily as possible, even if it cost considerable money.

Under the influence of these conditions the Derby cabinet, which came to power in June, 1866, proposed a renewal of the discussion as to arbitration. Lord Stanley, the foreign secretary, avowed a willingness to submit to an arbiter the question whether the British Government was so far responsible for the depredations of the *Alabama* as to be bound to pay the claims of those whose property was destroyed by the cruiser. He declined absolutely, however, to include in submission to the arbiter the question as to whether the recognition of the Confederacy as a belligerent on May 13, 1861, was justifiable. As Seward was tenacious on this point and insisted that the conduct of Great Britain as a whole should go into the determination of her responsibility for the cruisers, arbitration failed again to be adopted as the way out of the difficulties.

To the anxiety of the British cabinet to reach a settlement was added in 1867 a growing eagerness on the part of Secretary Seward to make such a settlement the capstone of his long public service, now approaching its end. Stimulated by these forces, diplomacy overcame the obstacles that had seemed insuperable. In 1868, after Charles Francis Adams had been succeeded as minister by Reverdy Johnson, a general agreement on all the matters at issue between the governments was slowly worked out. The Irish trouble was first cleared away by a protocol, eventually amplified into a treaty, assuring to naturalized citizens of the United States, though originally British subjects, the full rights in Great Britain of native-born citizens of the United States, that is, recognizing the right of expatriation for which the American Government had long contended. A second protocol referred to arbitration a boundary dispute in the far northwest that had been pending since the last years of Buchanan's administration. The third and last of the agreements, the ill-fated Johnson-Clarendon convention signed January 14, 1869, provided for the *Alabama* claims.

In this convention the controverted issues as to belligerency and neutrality during the war were hidden away in a series of general provisions for the settlement of all claims upon either government for money compensation to citizens of the other, on account of transactions since 1853. A commission of four members,

two appointed by each government, was intrusted with the power to pass upon the claims
by majority vote.  When no majority should
be obtainable an umpire should be selected, if
necessary by lot; or, upon the demand of two
commissioners, the umpire should be the head
of a foreign state, to be agreed upon by the two
governments.

In this convention the British Government
yielded all that which it had hitherto held to be
impossible.  Both its administration of its neutrality laws, which Russell refused to regard as
arbitrable, and its recognition of Confederate
belligerency, which had been reserved by Stanley, were subject to the judgment of the arbiter
under the Johnson-Clarendon treaty; for in the
consideration of every claim the commissioners
and the umpire were directed to base their
decisions on the official correspondence of the
two governments, together with one oral argument on each side and such papers as the governments should choose to submit.  So far as
concerned the *Alabama* claims, these provisions
put before the tribunal every aspect of the long
controversy.

There was, however, little hope, from the
outset, that the concessive attitude of Great

Britain would bring the desired settlement. The internal political conditions in America were decidedly unpropitious. A presidential election in November of 1868 resulted in the choice of General Grant to succeed Andrew Johnson in the following March. There was extreme antipathy, personal and partisan, between the outgoing and the incoming administrations, and nothing so dear to Seward's heart as ratification of his final treaty could be anticipated. More than this, there was a widespread feeling in the United States that the offence of Great Britain was not of a kind to be expiated by the mere compensation of private individuals for financial losses. Seward had once instructed Adams that the conduct of Great Britain during the war must be regarded as "a national wrong and injury to the United States," for which indemnity to private citizens would be only the lowest form of satisfaction. The spirit of this declaration was not reflected in the Johnson-Clarendon convention, and the omission had much to do with the fate of the agreement. On the 13th of April, 1869, the Senate of the United States refused its consent to the ratification of the treaty by a vote of forty-four to one.

The practical unanimity of this vote was even less significant than certain incidents that accompanied the Senate's action. Though the session in which the treaty was considered was, as usual in such cases, secret, the Senate made public the speech of Senator Charles Sumner, chairman of the Committee on Foreign Relations, whose views thus were impressed with a quasi-official character. In this speech Sumner rehearsed the tale of British unfriendliness to the United States during the war, much as it had been told often in the despatches of Seward and Adams. A shifting of emphasis by the senator, however, impressed a new character upon the discussion. He put in the foreground of his complaint the charge that the course of the British Government had been a wrong to the American nation, bringing upon it suffering and humiliation in addition to vast expense; yet for this public and notorious wrong to a friendly and kindred people no intimation or expression of regret had come from Great Britain. The injuries sustained by the United States could not be measured, Sumner argued, by the losses of individuals, nor be compensated by payments to individuals. British responsibility was to the American nation, and was not to be limited by the property destroyed by the Confederate cruisers. As grounds for national claims against Great Britain that were not to be ignored in any satisfactory settlement, Sumner included the shrinkage of the American mercantile marine through the transfer of vessels to the British flag for protection against the cruisers; the rise in the cost of marine insurance; and the cost of the war for the two years by which it was estimated to have been prolonged through the acts and negligence of the British Government. As to the money reckoning of the claims thus set forth, Sumner admitted that a figure was difficult to arrive at. The direct losses by the destruction of private property he thought might total some $15,000,000; for the indirect losses the suggestions that he made pointed to a sum of many hundred millions.

Sumner's speech was received with vociferous joy by all the Anglophobes in the United States. The Fenians were deeply gratified with his exposure of British treachery, and prepared with eagerness for the revenge that they thought must be exacted. The great mass of average citizens whose antipathy to the British had been dulled by the lapse of years since the war, were stirred with the ancient wrath through the artful and eloquent recital of the old tales of wrong. The effect of Sumner's speech was magnified on both sides of the Atlantic by the fact that he had always been reckoned the chief among the small number of friends of England in American public life. That he should now be hailed in the United States as the leader of the Anglophobes, threw his English admirers into consternation that was almost comical in its intensity. His suggestion of claims that would run up into the hundred millions was unsparingly denounced by all organs of British public opinion, and it proved a serious obstacle to the continuation of diplomatic discussion of the general question. There is little doubt, on the other hand, that the emphasis that he laid on what he called the national claims and on the national sense of injury received, as distinct from individual losses, was an important influence in determining the form of the ultimate settlement.

Sumner's attitude was, in fact, the outcome of a deliberate purpose, for which British radical politics was in some degree responsible. We have seen that for several decades the feeling had been common and unconcealed in high quarters that the colonies were a burden to

Great Britain and should be got rid of as soon as possible. Sumner's relations with Cobden and Bright, the most convinced advocates of this policy, made it very familiar to him. It was to Cobden's speeches, indeed, that Sumner was indebted for the catalogue of the national losses for which he held the British Government responsible. The great free-trader, when assailing the conduct of the Palmerston-Russell cabinet during the war, set forth in full detail the damage to the American merchant marine due to that conduct, and was scarcely less specific than Sumner in justifying a claim by the United States for reparation. In 1869 Cobden was dead, but John Bright and other radicals were in the Gladstone cabinet, and the prime minister himself was well over toward the radical wing of the liberal line. Sumner's purpose, then, was to use Cobden's views on the *Alabama* claims to promote his views as to the colonies. The senator would put the claims at so enormous a figure as to make the settlement of them impossible except by turning over to the United States all the British possessions in the Western Hemisphere. Such was the proposition that he later advised Secretary Fish to make the basis of all further negotiation, adding the profound suggestion that this simple expedient would remove for all time the tension on the Canadian frontier due to the activities of the Fenians.

This project of Sumner's is illuminating as to the practical quality of his statesmanship. He assumed that the dismemberment of the British Empire, because it was considered as an ideal by politicians concerned in the internal problems of England, could be demanded with impunity by a foreign power as a sort of war indemnity for a purely constructive war.

Hamilton Fish became secretary of state in the spring of 1869, and devoted himself from the outset to a serious but not ostentatious effort to overcome the ill effects of Sumner's speech and bring the negotiations back to at least as hopeful a situation as that in which Seward had left them. The Gladstone cabinet, with Lord Clarendon at the Foreign Office, was as eager as Fish to work toward an adjustment. On both sides, however, the difficulties were great. British susceptibilities had been so outraged by Sumner's extravagant demands that any sign of concession to them by Clarendon would destroy the Gladstone government. On the other hand, American popular sentiment was keyed up to the pitch set by Sumner, and the senator's influence had to be reckoned on in opposition to any abatement of the extreme national claims. Nearly two years of secret and unofficial negotiations were necessary before a plan of adjustment was hit upon that could be allowed to take official shape. In the interval the stars in their political courses had fought for harmony. Sumner, through a violent personal and political quarrel with President Grant, lost his influence with the supporters of the administration, and was eventually deposed from his powerful position as chairman of the Senate Committee on Foreign Relations. The Franco-Prussian War, with its cloud of threatening diplomatic questions on the Continent, gave a fresh impulse to the desire of the British leaders to be free from the harassing burden of American unfriendliness. Under these conditions the agreement was reached for the appointment of a joint high commission to meet at Washington and provide by treaty for the settlement of all the matters in controversy between the two governments. This commission, after deliberations lasting from February 27 to May 8, 1871, concluded on the latter date the Treaty of Washington that constitutes a noteworthy landmark in the history of Anglo-American relations.

In the forty-two articles of the treaty were embodied provisions for the settlement of the *Alabama* claims; of other claims by British and American citizens arising out of the Civil War; of the various controversies between the United States and British North America—as to the inshore fisheries, navigation, and commerce—left pending by the abrogation of the Reciprocity Treaty in 1866; and finally of the dispute as to the ownership of the island of San Juan, at the far western end of the line fixed by the Oregon Treaty of 1846.

As to the *Alabama* claims, the agreement embodied in the treaty signified great concessions on both sides in the interest of an amicable settlement. Great Britain expressed regret "for the escape, under whatever circumstances, of the *Alabama* and other vessels from British ports, and for the depredations committed by those vessels." In addition to this soothing admission that something disagreeable had happened to the United States, the British Government consented to arbitration in the fullest sense in reference to all the claims. Three rules were laid down as to the duties of a neutral government, and the arbitral tribunal was enjoined to base its judgment on these rules, though the British Government recognized them, not as a statement of principles of international law in force in 1861–5, but as principles that ought in the future to be adopted by maritime powers, and that Great Britain had, in fact, sought to live up to during the American war. The three rules defined the duty of a neutral government, in respect to the fitting out and supplying of war-ships, in such terms as to make it morally certain that judgment would be adverse to Great Britain on the case of the *Alabama,* if not as to other of the Confederate cruisers. The British Government, in short, not only assumed a somewhat apologetic attitude at the outset, but also submitted to be judged by principles that were not obligatory as rules of international conduct at the time of the acts concerned, and that insured an unfavorable decision. A proud and powerful nation does not put itself in such a position without potent motives. One such was obvious and unconcealed: the general adoption of rigorous rules of neutral duty would be very advantageous to Great Britain whenever she should become a belligerent. More influential than this selfish interest, however, was the desire, in no small measure purely sentimental, to be on friendly terms with the United States. The American democracy had proved in the severest of tests its fitness to survive, and the homage of a people and a generation in whom Darwinism was taking deep root was generously bestowed on the people who so opportunely illustrated the dogma of science.

Not all the concession in the Treaty of Washington was on the part of the British. One point that had been strenuously insisted on as the original grievance of them all by Secretary Seward and Mr. Sumner was allowed by Secretary Fish to recede quietly into the background. This was the premature recognition of the Confederacy as a belligerent. Fish took the position that this action of the British Government was evidence of an unfriendly spirit, but could in no sense be the ground of a claim for compensation. This admission was regarded as having a bearing on the general question of the national or indirect claims. These were not the subject of any reference or allusion in the treaty, and it was understood by the British negotiators that the American Government had definitely abandoned them, as it

was known to have ignored the demand of
Sumner that a withdrawal of the British flag
from the Western Hemisphere should be a preliminary condition to any settlement whatever.
As a matter of fact, the Americans had no
desire to urge the extravagant claims that
Sumner had made so conspicuous.  The British
commissioners, on their side, were without authority to consider them.  Yet because popular feeling was so sensitive about them on both
sides of the water the negotiators avoided all reference to them, and by this very excess of caution
left room for a dangerous misunderstanding.

The tribunal of arbitration met and organized at Geneva, Switzerland, in the middle of
December, 1871.  It consisted of five arbitrators, appointed respectively by the governments of the United States, Great Britain,
Italy, Switzerland, and Brazil.  The cases of
the two contending governments were at once
presented in printed form.  That of the United
States was found to include, in addition to the
claims for losses due to the destruction of vessels by the cruisers and to the pursuit of the
cruisers, claims also for the loss involved in the
transfer of the merchant marine to the British
flag, the increased cost of insurance, and the

prolongation of the war. That is, the indirect
or national claims were laid before the tribunal
along with the rest. Protests arose at once
from every organ of opinion in Great Britain.
To admit responsibility for that kind and degree
of loss would mean, it was declared, national
humiliation and financial ruin. The government and the negotiators contended that the
wording of the treaty excluded the indirect
claims from submission to the tribunal, and that
such exclusion had been agreed to in conference
by the American negotiators. The latter denied any such agreement or interpretation.
Great Britain stood firm in her contention,
however, and her agent was directed to withdraw from the arbitration in case consideration
of the indirect claims should be persisted in.
After many months of tension and of deep distress among the friends of peace and amity, a
way out of the *impasse* was found that was
acceptable to both parties. The tribunal itself
declared that it did not consider itself authorized, under international law, to award money
compensation for such losses as those involved
in the indirect claims. The American agent
thereupon refrained from demands upon the
arbiters for further attention to these claims.

This happy outcome of the dispute was quite as pleasing to the American as to the British Government. Fish and his coadjutors had no expectation or desire that Great Britain should be mulcted in consequential damages. Sumner's speech had created a surprisingly strong sentiment in support of such mulcting, and it was problematical whether the administration could afford, in the year of a presidential election, to run counter to this sentiment. Animosity toward the Southerners was at this time a strong factor in the politics of the Republican party, and it fell in well with this feeling to disparage the South by contending that the remarkable prolongation of its resistance to the North was due solely to the aid it received from Great Britain. The rejection of the indirect claims by the tribunal of arbitration itself relieved the administration of all responsibility for abandoning them, and passed without noteworthy effect on American public opinion.

The judgment of the tribunal needs but casual mention. In respect to three of the Confederate cruisers, the *Alabama*, the *Florida*, and the *Shenandoah*, Great Britain was found to have contravened the three rules of neutral conduct laid down by the treaty, and the damages

due to the United States on account of the
dereliction were assessed at $15,500,000. Sir
Alexander Cockburn, the British arbitrator,
dissented from the judgment of the tribunal on
all but a single point, namely, that due diligence had not been used in ascertaining the
character of the *Alabama* and preventing her
departure from Liverpool. The dissenting opinions of the Englishman were embodied in a very
lengthy document, in which he expressed with
unjudicial candor his contempt for the intelligence of his fellow arbitrators and for the methods and attainments of those who conducted
the American case. Cockburn's caustic criticism found some reflection in the Tory press,
and there appeared more or less of the once
familiar diatribe against the Yankees. In general, however, the judgment was acquiesced
in by British public opinion with good grace.
Even Cockburn ended his offensive opinion with
an expression of the hope and desire that the
arbitration would prove a potent influence in
maintaining amity between the two kindred
peoples.

This was indeed the dominant note in Great
Britain. The whole social and political movement of the day, with the now liberalized Glad-

stone in the lead, was in the democratic direction. Following the extension of the suffrage to the lower classes came the adoption of the secret ballot, to secure the independence of the new voters; and a great increase of state and rate supported education, to promote intelligence among them. Aristocratic privilege was summarily suppressed in one of its most cherished strongholds by the abolition of the purchase of commissions in the army. Disestablishment of the Irish church, and the Irish Land Act of 1870, whatever other factors played a part in their enactment, were for the benefit of the masses as against the classes. In the support that Mr. Gladstone derived from public opinion for all these great measures it is quite impossible that no influence was traceable to the example of the American democracy, now so recently triumphant over the dangers that had been considered certain to insure its ruin. Conservatism could no longer point a warning finger, as in the early days of the war, to the fate of a nation that should follow American examples. France also just at this time renewed her republican experimentation, and furnished the world again with illustrations of the working of popular government. In England, however, only the "blind hysterics of the Celt" were discernible across the Channel, and the gaze must follow the trail of the Anglo-Saxon across the ocean to rest on anything really trustworthy.

In the United States the announcement of the actual award attracted little attention or comment. It came in the midst of a heated electoral campaign, and was little available for partisan purposes. The Treaty of Washington had afforded to the Americans their most substantial victory a year earlier, when Great Britain expressed her regret and agreed to arbitration. The carrying out of the treaty was followed with the somewhat languid interest of him who gathers up the trophies after the victory is won.

Before the expiration of the year 1872 another trophy dropped quietly into the hands of the United States. The Treaty of Washington provided for the settlement of the San Juan water boundary by the arbitration of the German Emperor. By the treaty which ended the Oregon dispute in 1846 it was provided that the line between the United States and British America should be the forty-ninth parallel of latitude from the Rocky Mountains to "the

middle of the channel which separates the
continent from Vancouvers Island, and thence
southerly through the middle of the said channel . . . to the Pacific Ocean." The channel
in question was at one place about fifty miles
wide and filled with islands, among which
several navigable passages trending southward
were discernible. The dispute was as to which
of these passages was the "channel" through
which the boundary passed. The island of San
Juan, occupied since 1859 by detachments of
both American and British troops, would belong
to the one country or the other according to
the result of the dispute. In October, 1872, the
German Emperor rendered a decision sustaining the contention of the United States and
assigning the island thus to the Americans.

Two other arbitral procedures must be mentioned before the unique achievement of the
Treaty of Washington in this field is exhausted.
One arose under the provision in the treaty for
the adjudication by a commission of all Civil
War claims, other than those known as the
*Alabama* claims, for compensation by either
government for losses sustained through its
acts by citizens of the other. In the negotiation of this provision Great Britain agreed that

no claim based on the loss of slaves by a British subject should be presented. On the other hand it asked that the losses sustained by Canadians through the Fenian raids should be passed upon by the commission. This the Americans refused to concede, and the British withdrew the demand. What actually came before the commission was chiefly a large mass of claims by British subjects for the seizure or destruction of their property incidentally to the military operations on land and to the blockade of the coast. A few claims against Great Britain were presented by Americans for losses sustained in the operations of the Confederates in Canada in raids across the frontier. The commission, on which the position of umpire was held by the Italian minister at Washington, rendered its final judgment in September, 1873. All the claims by Americans were dismissed, and out of the 478 claims by British subjects 181 were allowed, with awards totalling something over $1,900,000.

The last of the arbitral proceedings provided for in the Treaty of Washington related to the familiar old matter of the inshore fisheries. We have seen that the much-prized privilege of fishing within the three-mile line was con-

ceded to the Americans by the Reciprocity
Treaty of 1854 in return for the free admission
of leading Canadian products into the United
States, and that the privilege expired with the
abrogation of the treaty in 1866. Friction between the American fishermen and the authorities of the Maritime Provinces, such as had been
common and troublesome prior to 1854, made its
appearance again after 1866. Efforts to read-
just things on the basis of tariff concessions, as
in the Reciprocity Treaty, failed before the
uncompromising refusal of the Americans to
modify their duties. In the Treaty of Washington an agreement was reached through the
offer of the Americans to pay for the privilege
of the inshore fishing in hard cash. This proposition was accepted, but the negotiators were
quite unable to get together on the amount that
should be paid. This question, therefore, was
left to arbitration. The treaty provided that
the inshore fisheries should be open to the
Americans, and, on the other side, that Canadian
fish and fish-oil should be admitted duty-free
to the United States. This arrangement was
to last for ten years, after which it was subject
to termination on two years' notice by either
party. The task of the commission of arbitra-

tion was, therefore, to determine how much cash, if any, in addition to the free admission of fish and fish-oil, would make a fair compensation for the privilege of the inshore fishing. The commission to whom the matter was referred made its decision at Halifax on November 23, 1877, and awarded $5,500,000 in gold to Great Britain. This award was regarded as excessive and unfair by many well-informed persons in the United States, and its validity was questioned on technical grounds by some; but the government duly paid the sum and closed the incident.

This Halifax commission completed the remarkable series of judicial proceedings of an international character through which the jolts and displacements caused by the Civil War were corrected and compensated, and the relations of the English-speaking peoples were restored to the plane of official and, in a greater degree than ever before, of real amity. The adjustment in respect to the fisheries was, of course, less closely and exclusively than the other arbitrations related to the Civil War. The difficulty that made the issue was destined to remain, as it had been for a century, a source of irritation and disturbance for an indefinite future. It afforded at this time, as it had afforded earlier, and would afford later, a transition topic from controversies in which the mother-country was the chief protagonist against the United States to those in which the British-American provinces held the leading position. Not the least important of the results which are traceable in a distinct if not a wholly decisive way to the influence of the desperate war in the United States, was the great political transformation in British America made effective by the creation of the Dominion of Canada in 1867. This was a capital event in the history of the relations of the English-speaking peoples of the earth and to it our attention must be for a time directed.

# CHAPTER VI
## THE GROWTH OF CANADA AND ITS PROBLEMS

In the proceedings that resulted in the Treaty of Washington of 1871 an important part was played by two prominent Canadians. Sir John Rose was the confidential agent of the British cabinet in the twenty months of secret diplomacy at Washington through which negotiation of the treaty was made possible; Sir John A. Macdonald was one of the five British members of the joint high commission by which the treaty was actually concluded. Rose had been until very recently minister of finance in the Canadian cabinet; Macdonald was the prime minister of the Dominion. The participation of Rose in the affair was determined largely by his exceptionally wide and intimate business and social connections in all three of the countries concerned, and by his amiable personality; the appointment of Macdonald signified the formal recognition by Westminster that the British-American commonwealth was entitled

to share through its government in the imperial
diplomacy that affected it.  Complaints had
always been made by the colonials that their
interests were lightly regarded in the adjustments reached between the British Government
and the United States.  A Canadian representative in the negotiations would shield the government against such complaints, though, as
Sir John Macdonald shrewdly foresaw, colonial
wrath, if things went wrong, would not again
be dissipated in long-range fretting against
Westminster, but would fall with concentration
and promptness upon his own devoted head.
Despite the suspicion that his function might
be primarily that of the scapegoat, he served
on the joint high commission with force and
efficiency, and strengthened *pro tanto* the prestige at home and abroad of the recently organized Dominion of Canada.

The union of all the British provinces of
North America in a single governmental system
had been contemplated as possible and desirable
by thoughtful publicists for many decades.
With the increase of population, the growth of
intercourse, commercial and social, and the improvements in means of communication, the
advantages of union became ever more percep-

tible. The impulse to its actual realization
came, however, as much from without as from
within the provinces. It was not a mere coincidence that the initial steps toward creating
the Dominion of Canada were taken during the
Civil War in the United States.

Sympathy in Canada with the South was
sufficiently common and sufficiently outspoken
during the war to evoke much heated denunciation across the border. With the rumors
and realities of extensive operations by the Confederates from a base in Canada, the temperature
of Northern comment became excessively high.
The attitude of the Canadian authorities remained scrupulously correct, and the excitement
pervading the press and platform of the North
was properly discounted; yet there remained a
feeling of uneasiness and foreboding as to what
was going to happen when the titanic struggle
should end. If the North should triumph, a
war of revenge against Great Britain and its
possessions was likely; if the North should fail,
an effort to compensate for the loss of the South
by expansion at the expense of Great Britain
might equally be expected. In either case it
behooved the prudent statesman to take all
possible precautions for the care of the provin-

cial interests. Some kind of consolidation was obviously desirable for the security of the half dozen all but independent political organisms that made up British North America.

It so happened that just at this time the legislative union by which Upper Canada and Lower Canada had been brought into harmony in 1841 reached the end of its usefulness. Party conflict, turning upon the antipathy between the French and the English races, brought paralysis upon the administration. A way out could not be found till a coalition of the dead-locked parties was effected for the purpose of instituting a new constitutional system through federation. The specific requirement in the internal politics of Canada was some readjust-ment that should satisfy the demands of the English element in the upper province for power proportioned to their now superior numbers as compared with the French of the lower prov-ince. Failure to satisfy these demands was likely at any moment to cause a revival of the sentiment in favor of annexation to the United States. The Americans were manifestly re-solved upon abrogating the Treaty of Reci-procity, in order to renew the commercial pres-sure upon the Canadians, at the same time that

the bitterness of the war-time was making a
resort to arms far from improbable. Under
these circumstances all the statesmen and other
classes who were devoted to the British connection were stimulated to strenuous action.

The Maritime Provinces meanwhile had been
for some years discussing the idea of a union
among themselves. Their motives were in some
measure the same as those that were operative
in Canada, and in some respects peculiar to
themselves. A conference on the subject between delegates from New Brunswick, Nova
Scotia, and Prince Edward Island took place in
1864, just at the time when the political situation in Canada was most critical. The Canadian ministry, a coalition of George Brown,
the ablest Radical, and John A. Macdonald, the
astute Conservative leader, seized the opportunity and effected the transformation of the
conference of the Maritime Provinces into a
more comprehensive body in which delegates
from Canada and Newfoundland were included.
The larger conference met at Quebec in October,
1864, and formulated a series of resolutions out
of which, after long and varied discussion in
each province and at London, was shaped the
constitution of the Dominion of Canada. The

British North America Act, in which this constitution found legal expression, was enacted
by the British Parliament in 1867, and the new
system went into operation on the 1st of July
of that year. The acceptance of the new order
by Canada was prompt and easy. To the other
provinces, however, the appeal of the confederation was far less strong. New Brunswick and
Nova Scotia acceded only after a sharp conflict,
and after the Fenian forays of 1866 accentuated
the arguments of the reformers. Prince Edward Island held aloof from the union until 1873,
while Newfoundland persisted permanently in
her independence.

A strong and conspicuous influence of the
United States in the formation of the Dominion
was to be seen in the distrust and fear that the
great republic inspired; yet this was by no
means the whole of the part played by the
greater nation in the self-realization of the less.
The constitutional problems of federal union
that confronted the Canadians were in most
cases those that had been the core of American
history since 1776. Hence throughout the debates in which the constitution of the Dominion
took form, the experience of the United States
was continuously before the debaters. Amer-

ican history and institutions were as sedulously
searched as those of the mother-country for
precedent and for warning.  Despite the unfriendly feelings in which the Dominion took
its rise, its constitution is in the fullest sense an
embodiment of the combined experience of all
three of the great English-speaking peoples of
the day.

In the project for the union of the British
provinces was involved the larger project of a
national consolidation of the whole of the British territory in America north of the United
States.  In correspondence with the expansion
of the republic across the continent to the
Pacific, the new Dominion was to include the
whole vast region westward to the ocean and the
Russian boundary.  Nor was the slow and pain-
ful process through which the United States had
acquired its western area to be duplicated.  The
course of the imperial government was definitely agreed upon before the British North
America Act was passed.  In 1868 the rights
of the Hudson's Bay Company, in whom up to
1859 the sole control of most of the region had
for generations been vested, were taken over
by the Dominion.  Three years later the province of Manitoba was organized on part of this

territory as a new member of the confederation, and still another province, British Columbia, far across on the Pacific, also entered the Dominion. Thus emulously the new English-speaking nation duplicated, with whatever disproportion in numbers, the westward progress of its great neighbor on the south. The faithfulness of the duplication unhappily extended to certain unsavory details of politico-financial operations in the development of the new regions. In the United States the first transcontinental railway was completed in 1869. In Canada the pledge of immediate and energetic prosecution of a parallel enterprise was a feature of the procedure through which British Columbia became a part of the Dominion. A single year, 1873, witnessed in its early months the ruin of several fair political reputations in the United States by the malodorous exposure of the Credit Mobilier, and in its later months the downfall of the first prime minister of the Dominion in consequence of relations with the financiers of the inchoate Canadian Pacific enterprise.

The consolidation of British North America into the Dominion was in itself an expression of the feeling of national unity, and it was followed by the steady unfolding of policies that were in harmony with that ideal. Nationality, as a basis of political organization, has been historically a concept quite free from the limitations of exact definition. Community of ancestry, of language, of traditions, of customs, of religion, of geographic environment, of economic interest, and of intellectual ideals have been jointly and severally set up as the essential justification for the claim to the rights and privileges of a nation. No one of these could be predicated of the Dominion of Canada in 1867. Under such circumstances it was no light undertaking for the 3,500,000 scattered people of the provinces to set out on the way of self-sufficiency. The initial requirements of the enterprise were obviously the assurance of political and economic independence of the United States and the maintenance at all hazards of the connection with the United Kingdom. Awkward questions were involved from the outset in these requirements, but they were met with boldness and success.

The constitution of the Dominion dealt with the most rancorous problems of race and religion by disjoining the two old provinces of Canada and giving to each—Protestant and English Ontario and Catholic and French Que-

bec—a complete government of its own, subject to the supremacy of the government of the
Dominion. To counteract the well-nigh overwhelming economic pressure by which commerce
and industry were made subject to the United
States, every effort was put forth to develop
railways running east and west. The Inter-
colonial Railway, uniting Quebec with Halifax,
a long-projected enterprise of both economic
and military importance, was completed with
imperial aid in 1876. The Canadian Pacific,
delayed by the scandal of 1873, was not in operation until nearly ten years later than the Inter-
colonial. Along with these great monuments
of national growth came the slow but sure development of that system which has been a
feature of every new birth of national spirit
in the nineteenth century—the stimulation of
industry by a protective tariff. In 1878 Sir
John A. Macdonald, after five years of exclusion from power following his downfall on the
Canadian-Pacific affair, won a great popular
triumph on the clearly defined issue of protection, and at once put the new policy into
operation. The United States was just at this
time emerging from the fiscal chaos of the Civil
War. Specie payments superseded the irre-

deemable paper currency, and the refunding of the huge war debt rendered possible far-reaching readjustments in revenue and taxation. This situation brought the question of the tariff to the foreground in politics and demanded the judgment of the people as to maintaining the high protection that had been established through the fiscal exigencies of the war. Though the principle was less decisively settled for many years than in the Dominion, the practical issue was the same. As Canada introduced the protective tariff, the United States retained it.

Thus by the opening of the ninth decade of the century the two English-speaking peoples of America had reverted to the restrictive commercial and industrial system that had been dropped with much parade of finality in the fifth decade. Economic independence of Great Britain was the chief end that determined the policy of the United States; economic independence of the United States was the chief end that determined the policy of Canada. In each case the experiment was costly, but far more so to the Dominion than to the republic. No small sacrifice to the national ideal was required in resisting the lure of trade, transportation, and financial advantage to the southward and laboriously building up a purely Canadian economy. The spirit that sustains such sacrifices, however noble and exalted it undoubtedly may be in some aspects, is notoriously not the spirit that most promotes cordial friendships among neighboring peoples. The simultaneous renascence of protectionism in the United States and Canada had a very close relation to the friction that became spectacular in the eighties and the early nineties. The immediate source of the friction was the very familiar old question of the inshore fisheries on the Atlantic coast, with later a less familiar but no less troublesome dispute over the seal fisheries of the far northwestern ocean.

The Treaty of Washington of 1871, as we have seen, admitted Americans to the inshore fisheries on the coast of the Dominion, in return for the admission of fish and fish-oil free of duty to the United States and such additional compensation as should be awarded by arbitrators. This arrangement went into effect July 1, 1873, and a year later Newfoundland became a party to it. The award of $5,500,000 by the Halifax commission practically sounded the knell of this arrangement. The amount was deemed exorbitant by most Americans competent to judge, the position officially taken by the government being that the privilege of the inshore fishing was desirable for Americans, not at all for economic advantage, but merely to remove a cause of international friction. This latter purpose was not wholly achieved. In 1878, at Fortune Bay, Newfoundland, an American fishing crew was mobbed by local residents for disregarding the prohibition to ply the trade on Sunday. The British Government ultimately granted an indemnity to the Americans, but the question whether local provincial legislation was seriously to affect the rights based on treaties remained not altogether clear.

The definitive committal of both Canada and the United States to protectionism confirmed the fate of the fisheries arrangement. The fish-packing interests of New England entered strong and continuous protests against the sacrifice of their rights by the free admission of Canadian fish, while other products of the Dominion were subject to heavy duties. When the ten years expired for which the fisheries articles were to run, Congress, with little or no opposition, directed the President to give the requisite two years' notice of the abrogation of the articles. Accordingly, they ceased to be operative on July 1, 1885, and the way was open for renewal of the ancient friction. A provisional arrangement by which the Americans were not to be molested in their customary pursuits for the season of 1885 secured peace for that year; but with the next fishing-season troubles promptly developed that severely strained the resources of diplomacy. The authorities of the Dominion, in whose jurisdiction the police of the shores and the enforcement of the customs laws now lay, proceeded to a merciless enforcement of the rules that operated to hamper the enterprise of the American fishermen. Under these rules fishing-vessels were forbidden to enter Canadian territorial waters except for shelter, repairs, wood or water. Many a captain took the chances of trouble by seeking under cover of these exceptions to renew the supply of bait on which the success of his deep-sea fishing depended. The zeal of the Canadian guard-boats was as active as that of the American fishermen, and frequent seizures were made of the alleged offenders. Complaints and recriminations in the press and in the legislatures of the two countries assumed great scope and bitterness. It was charged in the United States that the sole animus of the Canadian procedure was the desire to force concessions to Canadian goods in the tariff. In Canada, on the other hand, it was charged that the agitation across the border was designed to break down the Canadian tariff in the interest of American manufactures. That there was an element of truth in both charges did not materially relieve the situation.

The tension due to this matter lasted till after the presidential election of 1888. Only the season of 1886, however, presented incidents of a really serious character. As a consequence of these incidents the American Congress, in its following session, enacted a retaliatory law, authorizing the President, in case of further ill treatment of the fishermen, to exclude from American waters and ports the vessels and commodities of the Dominion. No action was ever taken, however, under the authority conferred by this act. The lessons of 1886 produced a less militant attitude on the part of both the American fishermen and the Canadian revenue officers. Methods were devised through which the difficulties that arose between them could be and were promptly adjusted. Yet on account of the partisan political conditions prevailing, especially in the United States, the significance of every frictional episode was systematically exaggerated, and the permanent diplomatic settlement of all the controversies was prevented. A treaty was actually concluded, February 15, 1888, the terms of which provided a full and equitable provision for all the doubtful points that had arisen. The Senate of the United States refused to approve it, for reasons which, so far as the public debate on the question may be assumed to reveal them, related much more to President Cleveland's candidacy for re-election than to the merits of the fisheries question. Pending the action of the Senate, a *modus vivendi* for two years was agreed to by the governments, under the terms of which licenses to trade for fishing-supplies in the British ports were granted for a price to the American fishermen, and they were absolved from burdensome customs regulations. Though the treaty failed, the terms of this *modus* continued to govern the situation by the tacit consent of all the parties concerned, and further trouble was for the time avoided.

The friction after 1885 over the fisheries had far-reaching effects. It contributed to the development of an anti-British sentiment in the

United States that reached a serious climax a decade later. The feeling at first excited by the seizure of the American fishermen was directed naturally against the Canadians. Later, despite the unconcealed and eager efforts of the British imperial government to bring about a satisfactory accommodation, a truculent spirit in respect to England became increasingly manifest throughout the United States. It was wide-spread rather than deep, and it received nourishment from a number of casual circumstances.

The home politics of Great Britain contributed something. It was in 1886 that Mr. Gladstone's Irish policy wrecked the Liberal Party and brought Lord Salisbury in for a long tenure of the premiership. The Parnell movement for home rule had for years attracted much sympathy in the United States, even outside the circle of Irish-Americans from whom it drew so much of its financial support. When Gladstone gave way to the pressure of the Irish and introduced his first Home Rule Bill, the action presented itself to very many Americans as another step in the democratic direction which he had followed, notably in the extension of the suffrage in 1884. The failure

of the bill and the accession of the Marquis of
Salisbury to power appeared to denote a great
triumph of reaction. Lord Salisbury's reputation in America was that of a case-hardened
aristocrat, with no faculty of aristocratic reserve
when the caustic delineation of his adversaries
was concerned. His opinions and expressions
concerning the United States had been notoriously contemptuous. It was easy, therefore,
for those who were interested, to strengthen the
presumption that the British policy in the matter of the fisheries was but a manifestation of
the unfriendly spirit which the prime minister
was disposed to promote.

The same disturbing end was furthered by the
condition of party politics in the United States.
Control of the government was divided between
the two great parties. President Cleveland
was a Democrat; the Senate was by a small
majority controlled by the Republicans. In
the country at large the voters were very evenly
divided, and the struggle of the politicians for
the support of those whose preferences could
be influenced by anti-British prejudice was very
keen. As the campaign of 1888 approached,
President Cleveland, in a dramatic manner,
brought the tariff into the foreground as the

chief issue between the parties, and committed the Democrats to the policy of abolishing the protective system. The Republicans, adopting formally the defence of protection, strove with energy and much success to attach to their adversaries the odium of devotion to "British free trade." It was freely asserted that English manufacturers were actively assisting the Democrats. By a trick that anything above infantile sagacity would have detected, the British minister at Washington, Sir L. S. Sackville West, was actually induced to write a letter to an unknown correspondent advising him to vote the Democratic ticket as the most advantageous to British interests. At the climax of the campaign the letter was published and was hailed by the Republicans as conclusive proof of their allegations concerning the relations of the English with the Democrats. President Cleveland demanded the recall of Sackville West. Lord Salisbury refused. Thereupon the minister received his passports, and his post was left vacant for many months by his government. The Republicans, meanwhile, triumphed in the elections, and under the presidency of Mr. Harrison entered upon a policy of extreme and aggressive protectionism through the enactment of the famous McKinley Bill.

In addition to this policy, the Harrison administration brought to the front a personality which gave small promise of better relations with any foreign power. Mr. James G. Blaine became secretary of state. He brought to that office the reputation of one who would assert with exceptional vigor the rights and claims of the United States. His political following included a group of Irish-Americans to whom the separation of Ireland from Great Britain was an end that justified any means. His public career teemed with incidents that had rasped the feelings of Britons and Canadians as effectively as Lord Salisbury had rasped the Americans. The conjunction of these two men at the head of the foreign offices boded ill for amity among the English-speaking peoples.

It was expected that the accession of the Harrison administration would be followed by a renewal of the tension concerning the northeastern fisheries. Forebodings in this respect proved groundless. No settlement of the disputed questions of right was indeed arrived at, but careful and considerate conduct by both fishermen and authorities made serious clashes avoidable. On the other side of the continent, however, in the waters of the northern Pacific, a situation had arisen in which, with reversed rôles, Americans and Canadians were in dangerous controversy.

In the summer of 1886, at the very time when the Canadian revenue cutters were giving most trouble to the cod and mackerel fishermen of New England, American revenue cutters began to make trouble for the seal-hunters of British Columbia. The laws of the United States prohibited the killing of fur-seals in Alaska except by a company to whom the right had been leased of taking a limited number of skins, by carefully restricted methods, on the Pribilof Islands in Behring Sea. These islands were the resort of vast numbers of the animals each summer for breeding. Hunting of the seals on the high seas, beyond the three-mile line, was carried on actively by vessels of American, British, Japanese, and other nationalities. The methods employed by these deep-sea hunters were wasteful of seal life, and were alleged to be the chief cause of a great decline in the number of animals frequenting the breeding-grounds. At the instance of the company whose interests were thus threatened, the American authorities in Alaska proceeded to assert far-reaching powers for controlling the situation. In 1886 three, and in the next summer four, British sealers were seized by American revenue cutters in Behring Sea, at distances from the shore varying from fifteen to one hundred and fifteen miles, on the charge of violating the law forbidding the killing of seals in Alaska. The court of the district upheld the seizures and inflicted penalties on the crews of the vessels, taking the ground that Behring Sea was *mare clausum*, and that so much of it as lay to the eastward of the water boundary described in the treaty of cession by Russia was subject to the territorial jurisdiction of the United States.

Against this whole procedure the British Foreign Office entered vigorous protests. There was involved a claim to control over a stretch of open ocean some seven hundred miles in width—and that by a government which was vehemently objecting to the exercise on the Atlantic coast of like control over ocean spaces but a paltry forty miles wide. The administration at Washington refrained from pressing the contention on which the Alaskan court rested, and ordered the release of the seized vessels. On other grounds, however, the preservation of the seals from extinction was taken up as a duty of general concern to civilized nations, and on the proposition of Secretary Bayard a project of joint action for the protection of the seals was agreed to in its general features by the British and other governments. This plan looked to a prohibition of pelagic sealing in Behring Sea. Before the adjustment of the details could be perfected, in May, 1888, the negotiations were somewhat abruptly suspended by the British Government at the request of the Canadian authorities. The sealing interests of British Columbia had by this time impressed upon the Dominion government the fear that an important industry was about to be sacrificed for the benefit of an American monopoly. Pointblank issue was made against the claim that the Pribilof seal herd was seriously decreasing in numbers, and it was stoutly maintained that if there was any perceptible diminution, it was attributable to the methods of the American monopoly rather than to pelagic hunting.

To the disputes as to the facts was added, as an influence in the sudden change of attitude by the British, the coincident rejection by the American Senate of the draft treaty touching

the northeastern fisheries.[1]  Both controversies
thus went over to be taken up by the successor
of the Cleveland administration.  In this situation there was no room to question the importance of the Canadian governmental and unofficial sentiment.  Sir Charles Tupper, the
shrewd and experienced associate of Sir John
Macdonald in the Dominion cabinet, was a
member of the commission that negotiated the
unratified treaty of 1888, and was the official
through whom the communication was made
that put an end to the negotiations as to the
seals.  The oft-reiterated complaint that Canadian interests were sacrificed through failure of
the imperial government to make itself informed
about them could have no place in connection
with these incidents.  On the contrary, the
Americans manifested from time to time impatience and even stronger feeling because of
the time lost, as they declared, by the care of
the British Foreign Office to insure that its
every step should receive the *visé* of the Dominion cabinet.

In the summer of 1889 the activity of the
revenue cutters in Behring Sea, which was suspended during the preceding summer, was re-

[1] See above, p. 280.

sumed. Nine British sealers were visited and six of them were seized. This precipitated a fervid diplomatic correspondence between Secretary Blaine and Lord Salisbury. His Lordship stood firm on the ground that British vessels must not be molested on the high seas. The secretary, dropping the claim of *mare clausum*, justified the action of the United States on the ground that pelagic hunting under the circumstances was *contra bonos mores*—in contravention of the general interest and welfare of mankind—and was therefore to be suppressed, like piracy, without regard to the normal freedom of the seas. By degrees, however, the debate worked around to the proposal of arbitration, with a provisional cessation of the killing of seals. A *modus vivendi* was arranged for the seasons of 1891 and 1892, under which taking furs was prohibited, and experts were set to work to ascertain all the facts of the situation. Meanwhile a treaty of arbitration was signed February 29, 1892, and duly ratified.

The tribunal of arbitration consisted of two Americans, two representatives of Great Britain, and one member appointed by the French, the Italian, and the Swedish Governments respectively. It was entirely in keeping with the trend of imperial relations that one of the British representatives should be Sir John S. D. Thompson, Canadian minister of justice, and that the responsibilities of British agent should be assigned to Sir Charles Tupper. The tribunal met for its first session at Paris in February, 1893, and rendered its decision on the 15th of August following. On all the points formally submitted for adjudication the decision was adverse to the contention of the United States. It was held that that power, in taking over Alaska from Russia, acquired no exclusive jurisdiction in Behring Sea and no exclusive rights in the seal fisheries therein; and that the American Government had no right of protection or property in the fur-seals that frequented the Pribilof Islands when the animals were outside the three-mile limit. At the same time the tribunal formulated regulations and restrictions under which, for the preservation of the herd, pelagic sealing ought to be carried on, and these rules were duly enacted into law by both governments for their respective subjects. Thus the maintenance of *bonos mores* on the high seas was made a matter of international co-operation, while the American Government, for its ambitious undertaking to exercise that lofty function unaided, was obliged to pay something like half a million dollars in damages to the seized British sealers.

The settlement of this dispute by arbitration gave much satisfaction to the special friends of peace among English-speaking peoples. Not that the controversy over the seals had seriously threatened war. Feeling in relation to it, whether in governmental circles or in the public at large, never became generally bellicose in either Canada, Great Britain, or the United States. Yet it doubtless did contribute a share, however small, to the stimulation of the intense nationalistic susceptibilities that were manifest in both the Dominion and the republic.

Pride of strength and of achievement became peculiarly demonstrative in the United States during the decade of the eighties. The cause can be but uncertainly detected amid the obscurities of national psychology, but the effects are patent and unmistakable. Through press and pulpit and platform was revealed a consuming sense of power and a deep craving to make it felt, and to extort recognition of it from other peoples. For three decades the problems of slavery and civil war had absorbed the physical and intellectual strength of the nation.

These had passed and a new generation demanded new opportunities for testing its forces. The population exceeded 50,000,000; the material resources of the land were being revealed in ever-increasing variety and volume; by the progress of settlement the vast interior spaces of the continent were peopled and organized, till at the decade's end the full-fledged States of the Union stretched in unbroken series three thousand miles from ocean to ocean. It was an imposing political fabric, and the citizen who admired it from within might be pardoned for insisting on tributes of admiration from without.

This national pride found something of satisfaction during the eighties in the beginnings of a fleet that should conform to the standards of the time. Likewise expressive of the feeling was the popular approval of the policy which secured to the United States, after a somewhat acrimonious tilt with Germany, a substantial foothold in the far-distant Samoan Islands. This initial excursion into the field of extra-American dependencies was stimulated by the exciting competition during the preceding years between Great Britain and Germany for colonial possessions. Those who had confidence in

the future expansion of American commerce
were much irritated at the thoroughness with
which the most promising scenes of coming
trade and naval stations for its protection were
appropriated by the European rival powers.
Samoa at least was insured to the commerce of
the United States, and in that fact was a source
of small but sufficient comfort for those to whom
the future of the Philippines was darkness.

Additional stimulus to American sensibilities
was given by the movement for imperial federation that took shape and became prominent
throughout the British Empire during the
eighties. The chief impulse to this movement
came obviously enough from the expanding
activities of Russia in Asia and Germany in
Africa. British prestige and commercial interests were felt to be imperilled. The Indian
Empire might readily yield to the insidious
sapping of the Russians; the self-governing
colonies in Australasia and Africa might be
lured to seek through nominal independence a
real connection with Britain's latest commercial rival. In Australia notoriously, and in
other of the colonies with no less certainty, an
active fraction of public opinion favored severance, sooner or later, of the British tie. In

England itself, as we have seen, such severance had long been regarded in high political circles as inevitable and not wholly undesirable. Now, however, that the time seemed to be approaching for the realization of this predestined break-up, opposition became vigorously vocal in both colonies and mother-land. The Imperial Federation League, unofficially, and a succession of conferences under the auspices of the imperial and colonial governments, officially, instituted earnest discussion of the ways and means of maintaining the unity of the empire.

While the origin of this agitation was in conditions remote from America, the future of Canada and its relations with the United States became at once, when the problem was fairly posed, the central question of the debate. The immediate practical end that engaged the attention of the federationists was military and naval defence of the widely scattered members of the empire. Tariff arrangements that should promote a unifying tendency were also suggested. So soon as discussion of these ends touched Canada, her great neighbor to the southward became the subject of disquieting consideration. Defensive arrangements for New South Wales might suggest malevolent intentions on the part of Germany or France or Japan; the tariff of the Cape Colony might be directed against the intrusive competition of these or half a dozen other enterprising nations: but in connection with the Dominion of Canada military and commercial protection could refer primarily to no power save the United States. Hence it was that the animated discussion of imperial federation acted as a challenge to the militant national spirit in the republic. Incidents of normal national development in which the Canadians took justifiable pride—the suppression of the Riel uprising of 1885 by Dominion forces, the completion of the railway line from ocean to ocean in the same year, the great improvements in the canals, and the development of manufactures—were jealously regarded by sensitive Americans as so many steps toward the perfection of an imperial policy of hostility toward the United States.

The internal party politics of the Dominion presented certain incidents that served to confirm the unfriendly trend in American opinion. In the later eighties systematic agitation was begun by a small group of able men for a policy of commercial union, even if it should lead eventually to political union, between Canada

and the United States. The basis of the movement was the despair of ever securing otherwise such trade relations with the powerful
neighbor as would bring real prosperity to the
people of the Dominion. The rejection of
reciprocity of the old sort in 1888 and the
triumph of the protectionists in the presidential elections of that year were held to have
ended all hope of escaping the ruthless extinction of Canada's industrial independence. Without ill feeling toward the mother-land and without desire to sever the political ties uniting the
colony to her, the advocates of commercial
union frankly declared that to Canadians, as
conditions had developed, the economic burden of the British connection had become too
great to be borne. Goldwin Smith, the literary high priest of this creed, sustained it with
all the frigid doctrinaire logic of Manchesterism
in its best estate, contending that geography
made physically inevitable, and political economy made morally necessary, the annexation of
Canada to the United States. Federation with
the far-flung fragments of English-speaking
humanity was to him a ridiculous dream. The
Liberal Party in the Dominion, with its tradition of free trade, showed some tenderness for

the commercial-unionists, while Sir John Macdonald, leading the Conservatives, in his last campaign, gladly seized the opportunity to appeal once more to the sentiment of loyalty to Great Britain. The elections of 1891 gave him a final victory, and showed with quite adequate clearness that the Canadian people preferred to follow their feelings in the British Empire rather than their interests in the American Republic.

No great access of hostile feeling in the United States toward the Canadians was manifest as a result of this preference. It was regarded by many Americans as a natural and properly spirited response to the McKinley tariff of the preceding year. This law administered almost fatal blows to certain important Canadian industries, and it was accompanied by the rejection, so peremptory as to be almost insulting, of overtures from Canada looking to the renewal of reciprocity as in 1854. The McKinley Act in fact proclaimed a tariff war à outrance between the two neighbors, and the Canadian election of 1891 signified a readiness for the struggle. In the United States, however, there was halting and indecision. The elections of 1892 brought the Democrats again into power,

and the result was a renunciation of the Mc-
Kinley programme, with the modified tariff of
1894. This in turn was repudiated by the
voters, and in 1897 the Dingley Act brought the
definitive adoption of protection in its most
thoroughgoing form.

The shifting phases of the prolonged and
complex struggle in the United States produced
the results that are inevitable when the conflicts over trade and markets that used to con-
vulse the politics of monarchies are reproduced
in democratic states. Among the masses there
was but a dim perception of the real financial
and industrial interests that were at stake in
the discussions over the tariff rates. What
appeared clear to all, however, was that foreigners, especially the British, were in some way
seeking to get advantages over American com-
petitors. The merits of the case not being
intelligible, the average citizen could be moved
in his judgments only by the sense of an insidious and pernicious activity by foreigners directed against his countrymen.

Such was the contribution made by the
tariff controversies to the latent feeling of hostility in the United States toward all things
British as it existed in the later eighties and

early nineties. The unfavorable decision in
the fur-seal arbitration had a certain influence
of the same nature. Whatever the merits of
the case on the technical claims of the lawyers,
it was a game played in which the British won
and the Americans lost. To show too much
chagrin over the defeat must be avoided; but
to nourish a dislike of the victor and be vigilant
for a chance to get satisfaction was within the
reach of all.

It was a synthesis of the various elements of
popular feeling just noticed, supplemented by
the influence of conspicuous political personalities, that produced the astounding explosion of
1895 in relation to Venezuela.

# CHAPTER VII

## VENEZUELA—AND AFTER

IN June, 1895, after a Liberal interlude of nearly three years under Mr. Gladstone and Lord Rosebery, the British Government came once more into the hands of the Marquis of Salisbury, leading the coalition of Conservatives and Liberal-Unionists. It was destined to be ten years before another change of party control should take place, so thoroughly were the Liberals demoralized by the fall of Parnell and the retirement of Gladstone.

Lord Salisbury entered upon his administration with complete consciousness that the relations of Great Britain with the other powers of Europe would require the most absorbing attention. The harrying of the Armenians by the Turks was in full progress, disturbing the delicate adjustment made by the Conference of Berlin in 1878; in the Far East, Japan, fresh from her triumph over China, was confronting Russia in such a way as to raise pressing questions about British interests in that region;

Africa, from the Cape to Cairo, teemed with disquieting problems—with Kitchener just starting to redeem the Soudan, Italy on the verge of disastrous war with Menelik of Abyssinia, France and Germany, in the central and southern regions of the continent, watching the promise of trouble between the British and their Dutch and native neighbors. Intent on the possibilities in all these directions, his Lordship was probably much shocked to be confronted, only a few weeks after taking office, with a diplomatic communication that peremptorily diverted his attention to affairs in America. On August 7 Mr. Bayard, ambassador of the United States, presented to Lord Salisbury the celebrated note of Secretary of State Olney on the matter of the Venezuelan boundary.

The line separating British Guiana from Venezuela had never been determined. Negotiations touching the subject had been carried on by the Venezuelan and British Governments at intervals since early in the nineteenth century, but for various reasons without conclusive result. Beginning in the late seventies, Venezuela had pressed insistently for a submission of the question to arbitration. At the same time she had kept the Government of the

United States informed as to the situation, and had urged upon that government the duty of sustaining the demand for arbitration. The Venezuelan contention was that Great Britain, under cover of the uncertainty as to the boundary, was continually extending her settlements and her jurisdiction into the disputed territory, and was thus contravening the Monroe Doctrine. In the documents submitted to the United States by the Venezuelan authorities there was some evidence to support this view, and to sustain the charge that the British refusal to go to arbitration was animated by the purpose to delay a settlement until still larger areas of rich mineral land should be occupied by British subjects.

Successive administrations at Washington listened with friendly interest to the Venezuelan representations, but refrained from taking up the matter with the British Government, partly because it was the wish of the Venezuelans that the United States should be the umpire in case of an arbitration, and this would be rendered impracticable if the United States should commit herself in any degree to the Venezuelan interest at the outset. During the first term of President Cleveland, however, when the tension on the subject had become so acute as to result soon in the rupture of diplomatic relations between Venezuela and Great Britain, Secretary Bayard made a formal tender of good offices to the British Government, alluding in his despatch to the Monroe Doctrine. The tender was declined, with no overwhelming manifestation of gratitude on the part of Lord Salisbury, and with only the most vague and general indication of the British position. A year later, in 1888, upon a report that British mining operators were beginning work in parts of the disputed territory hitherto untouched, Secretary Bayard made another offer of mediation, but with no more success. Somewhat later, with the active interest of the American Government negotiations between Venezuela and Great Britain were resumed, but in 1893 they came to a full stop again on account of the old obstacle. Venezuela demanded arbitration on the full claims of both parties; Great Britain refused absolutely, as she had done since the middle of the century, to submit to an arbiter her title to certain regions that had long been occupied by British settlements. These regions were held to be sufficiently well determined by a line run by a surveyor named Schomburgk, and the territory within this Schomburgk line was declared to be the irreducible minimum of the British possessions. Only what lay beyond it could be made the subject of arbitration. Against this attitude of the British Government the Venezuelan Government entered solemn protests, and made passionate appeals for intervention to the United States.

Mr. Cleveland was at this time President, and Mr. Bayard was ambassador of the United States at London. All the influences expressive of the national self-consciousness, as noticed in the last chapter, were obtrusively active in the American Republic. At the very beginning of his term the President had antagonized the whole chauvinistic spirit by a summary reversal of his predecessor's policy looking to the annexation of the Hawaiian Islands, and by a disastrous attempt to restore the native monarchy which the American population of the islands had recently overthrown. To the enemies of the administration this somewhat humiliating episode gave the cue for incessant iteration of the charge that the President lacked the virile spirit that would give the nation its proper place among the powers. Various unimportant incidents, which might have been magnified

into demonstrations of aggressiveness in foreign
policy, were adjusted without excitement or
display; and this again was used to strengthen
the idea that nothing worthy of a great nation
was to be expected of Cleveland. Reference
to the Venezuelan dispute with Great Britain
was made in the President's annual message
to Congress in December, 1894, and Congress
later responded by a resolution urging that the
question be settled by arbitration; but the
general feeling in America was that, however
desirable such procedure was, no action by the
administration was to be expected.

Mr. Cleveland, meanwhile, reached the conclusion that peril to peace would result if the
boundary dispute remained longer unsettled.
Venezuelan complaints continued frequent and
shrill; reports of further encroachments by
the British in the gold-mining regions were
diligently circulated; and ominous indications
appeared in the American press of nervousness
lest the Monroe Doctrine were threatened with
infringement. It was resolved to bring the
affair to a head at once, and Secretary Olney's
despatch above referred to was the means
adopted. That the despatch was well calculated to effect the immediate end in view, could

hardly be questioned. It reviewed the course of the boundary dispute, in the sense, for the most part, of the Venezuelan representations; it asserted the interest of the United States in the controversy on the ground, first, of the general principles of international law, and second, of the long-established and often-proclaimed policy known as the Monroe Doctrine; it maintained that the British refusal to submit the question to arbitration might cover a process of aggression upon Venezuela that the United States could not tolerate; and it concluded with a demand for a definite decision as to whether the British Government would or would not submit the boundary question in its entirety to impartial arbitration.

The tone and temper of this communication were unusual and should have warned Lord Salisbury of an impending crisis. In connection with the Monroe Doctrine, in particular, Secretary Olney's pronouncements were startling. Among its implications were: that there must be no intrusion by any European power in the politics of any state of either North or South America; that any permanent political union between an American and a European state is unnatural and inexpedient; that the

United States is practically sovereign on the American continent, "and its fiat is law upon the subjects to which it confines its interposition." The challenge of such audacious and arrogant dogmas it was naturally difficult to resist, and Lord Salisbury was not of the temperament to ignore it. His response to Olney's despatch took the form of two notes of the same date, November 26, 1895. One was devoted to a demonstration that the Monroe Doctrine had no standing in international law; that Mr. Olney's version of its content and implications had never before been heard or dreamed of; that neither in the Monroe Doctrine nor elsewhere could the United States find warrant for the assertion of an interest in every boundary dispute between an American state and a European power; and that Great Britain would repel with emphasis and something of indignation Secretary Olney's sweeping assumption that her connection with her American colonies was unnatural, inexpedient, and destined to cease. In his second note Lord Salisbury reviewed the course of the controversy with Venezuela, presenting facts and considerations that for the first time gave to the British case a reasonable, if not wholly convincing, foundation. The conclusion of the note, however, embodied a reiteration of the old decision, not to submit to arbitration the claims to regions within the Schomburgk line.

If in substance and spirit Olney's note was startlingly new, the response of Salisbury was discouragingly old. If the changed position and aspirations of the United States were by the one put in so high relief as to be somewhat coarse and repulsive, they were by the other left wholly out of the modelling. If Olney brusquely voiced the feeling of the youth who had reached his majority and claimed a grown man's estate, Salisbury sounded the old Tory note of querulous impatience with the restless and innovating spirit of the immature. No doubt was left by the correspondence that the two great English-speaking peoples were diplomatically at the point of most serious tension.

President Cleveland's demand having been refused by the British Government, he referred the whole matter to Congress, laying before that body, on December 17, 1895, the despatches above referred to, with a message announcing his views as to the existing situation and as to the course that should be pursued by the United States. With regret that the British Government had declined to agree to the most satisfactory mode of ending the controversy with Venezuela, he declared that the right, the duty, and the interest of the United States required that it ascertain in some way what the true boundary was. Only thus could there be certainty that a strong European power was not encroaching upon and oppressing a weak American republic, and thus violating the Monroe Doctrine. He asked Congress, therefore, to provide for a commission to investigate the history and facts of the matter, and report what the true divisional line was between Venezuela and British Guiana. The line thus determined it would be the duty of the United States to maintain as the lawful boundary. Any appropriation of lands or exercise of jurisdiction by Great Britain in places thus decided to belong to Venezuela would be, Mr. Cleveland affirmed, a wilful aggression upon the rights and interests of the United States, to be resisted by every means in its power. And this belligerent attitude he confirmed beyond all misapprehension by the ominous words: "In making these recommendations I am fully alive to the responsibility incurred, and keenly realize all the consequences that may follow." Yet, he con-

cluded, "there is no calamity which a great
nation can invite which equals that which follows a supine submission to wrong and injustice
and the consequent loss of national self-respect
and honor beneath which are shielded and
defended a people's safety and greatness."

The shock that was propagated through the
English-speaking world, and far beyond its
bounds, by this message of President Cleveland
had no parallel since the seizure of Slidell and
Mason a generation in the past. Two facts
contributed much to the intensity of the disturbance. The existence of anything like a
serious difference between the British and the
American Government was absolutely unsus-
pected outside of a very small circle of public
men; and the President was believed by both
his friends and his foes to be so resolutely pacific
in his attitude that only the most imperious
exigency could change it. The message revealed a disagreement so grave as to have moved
even Mr. Cleveland to thought and speech of
war. Nor was anything reassuring to be found
in the action of Congress; for both houses,
without opposition, adopted the measure that
the President recommended, and with the new
year a commission of distinguished Americans

appointed by the President began its laborious task of determining the true divisional line between Venezuela and British Guiana.

It is agreed by persons experienced in earthquakes that this species of phenomenon includes distinct varieties, clearly marked off from one another by physical and psychological effects. The most destructive materially and most disturbing mentally is that known in unscientific parlance as the "twister." President Cleveland's message had all the effects of the twister. Materially there was a huge displacement of credits and securities in the financial markets. Psychologically there was manifest on both sides of the Atlantic great bewilderment and obfuscation, with strange distortions and incoherencies in the reasoning processes. American public opinion sustained with extraordinary emphasis and unanimity the President's assertion of the Monroe Doctrine and his belligerent attitude toward the violation of it by Great Britain. Every latent current of hostility to the British and all the springs of aggressive national consciousness united in an impressive flood of popular feeling. If the administration had had no other purpose than to evoke for the information of the world the visible spirit of the American

democracy, that purpose was fully achieved in
the first week succeeding the Venezuelan message. Then came the distortions and confusion
of the twister. It began to appear on calm reflection that, despite the stirring words at the
end of Cleveland's message, war with Great
Britain was neither declared nor imminent.
Whether or not the Monroe Doctrine applied to
the boundary dispute, no allegation was made
that the treasured doctrine had in fact been
violated. Peril to the honor and interests of
the United States was hypothetical, not actual;
and the warning of dire results to follow a certain contingency was to be effective only after
a body of historians and jurists should have
discovered a boundary line which in all proba-
bility was humanly undiscoverable. With the
due realization of these conditions the spirit of
militant Americanism receded into the depths
and, stronger and more self-confident for having been revealed in its full proportions, awaited
a more propitious season for asserting itself.

Among the English people, meanwhile, Cleveland's message and the manifestations of American feeling that followed it were received chiefly
with bewilderment and incredulity. That the
two governments should have reached in utter

secrecy the verge of war, was incomprehensible; that so grave a situation should be due to an obscure boundary dispute in one of the least important fragments of the empire, seemed grotesquely beyond the limits of belief. Some voices from the lurking-places of ancient Toryism were shrill with resentment and defiance toward the new display of Yankee insolence; but the great volume of opinion sounded the note of amazed regret that tension had arisen, and of eager confidence that its causes could be removed. While responsible politicians were appropriately reticent, men of light and leading in other fields pronounced with emphasis and iteration that war between the two great English-speaking nations was unthinkable. Authors, journalists, ministers of the Gospel, and business men demanded that a peaceful way out of the threatening difficulty should be promptly found. The enormous development in means of communication and thence in personal relationships between the two peoples made powerfully for amity. Where in the days of the *Trent* affair intimacies between Englishmen and Americans were numbered by dozens, thousands and myriads existed in 1896. Across the dividing Atlantic, therefore, sped by mail and by cable great streams of protest against rupture in fact or in feeling. Friendly responses from America came promptly in reassuring volume. Influential groups on both sides of the ocean demanded that, no matter how tight and tangled the knot made by diplomacy, it be opened by the methods of peace, not of war. Arbitration for the settlement of disputes between the kindred peoples became within a few weeks the theme of an extremely energetic and wide-spread agitation, guided by co-operating leaders of the intellectual classes of both nations.

While this unofficial sentiment was taking active shape, there was much uneasiness lest the diplomatists should not see their way, after so peremptory a disagreement, to a dignified resumption of intercourse about the Venezuelan question. A counter-irritant to oversensitiveness on this ground in the British Foreign Office was found in the acute conditions that arose in a far distant part of the empire less than a fortnight after Cleveland's disturbing message was published. Jameson's ill-starred raid into the Transvaal met its humiliating end on January 2, 1896, and on the following day the German Emperor's congratulatory despatch to the Boer

President was made known. The explosion of British wrath over this incident drove Venezuela and its boundary quite out of the range of popular interest. Yankee interference in South America excited mild regret; German interference in South Africa roused the fiercest fighting passion. Yet the attitude of the United States, however unimportant relatively, could not be ignored by a prudent foreign minister in the presence of threatening conditions nearer home. For this reason, perhaps, among others, Lord Salisbury met more than half-way the advances of the Cleveland administration toward further negotiation.

In the middle of January the American commission applied through Secretary Olney for documentary and other information on which Great Britain based its views as to the true divisional line between Guiana and Venezuela. Lord Salisbury furnished with enthusiasm all that his office possessed. At the opening of Parliament in February both he and Mr. Balfour, leader of the Commons, admitted the interest of the United States in the boundary question, and intimated the hope that diplomacy would achieve a settlement of the difficulty. At the same time his Lordship indicated a much

less intolerant attitude than before as to the
efficacy of arbitration in international differences. In accordance with the disposition thus
manifested, a suggestion from Mr. Olney that
negotiations be undertaken at Washington for
the settlement of the difficulty with Venezuela
was agreed to by the British Government, with
a voluntary expression of willingness to take up
the matter either with Venezuela or with the
United States acting as her friend. So full a
concession to the American view could not fail
to insure a pacific agreement. The negotiations were begun forthwith between Great Britain and America. The British abandoned their
insistence on a fixed line as the irreducible minimum of their territory, and accepted the submission of the whole claim of each power to
arbitration, with the proviso that actual occupation or control of any region for fifty years
should give title to either party. On this basis
a treaty of arbitration between Great Britain
and Venezuela was readily agreed to and duly
carried out. With this the matter of the
boundary passed out of concern in the relations of the English-speaking peoples.

In its broad character as a diplomatic episode
this whole affair stands as an assertion by the

United States and a recognition by Great Britain of a far wider interest and authority beyond her borders than was ever before definitely maintained by the American Republic, whether as Monroe Doctrine or otherwise. The giant democracy took her place among the great powers of the earth, whether for weal or for woe, and the British motherland was the first to accord recognition to the new position.

More than this, however, gives importance to the Venezuelan boundary controversy in the history of the relations of English-speaking peoples. Here began a systematic and comprehensive agitation for the definitive supplanting of war by arbitration as the last resort in the disputes among nations. The negotiation of the treaty by which the Venezuelan boundary was settled was accompanied by the framing of a general treaty of arbitration applicable for the future to controversies between Great Britain and the United States. The diplomats who in November and December of 1895 sent thrills of warlike feeling through a hundred million English-speaking people, in the spring of 1896 were meticulously intent on devising the formulas that should render war impossible. So far as this situation was a result of the disturbance caused by the presidential message of December 17, it impressively confirmed and justified the unwavering contention of Mr. Cleveland that that document was in purpose and effect a powerful factor in the maintenance of peace.

On January 11, 1897, three weeks before the conclusion of the treaty that sent the Venezuelan boundary to arbitration, Secretary Olney and Sir Julian Pauncefote signed at Washington a general treaty of arbitration. It embodied the closely reasoned conclusions of strong and sincere minds as to the best practical methods of solving the intricate problems presented by the end in view. All differences between the two governments that diplomacy should prove unable to adjust were to be sent to arbiters. Three kinds of tribunals were provided, among which the jurisdiction over the various classes of controversies was distributed, with provisions for appellate and revisory procedure. The tribunal whose function it was to deal with the delicate questions of territorial claims and of principles affecting "national rights" was to consist of three judges from the higher courts of each government, with no umpire, decisions to be valid only by a vote of at least five to one.

The provisions of this treaty proved to be in advance of effective public opinion in the United States. Distrust of Great Britain could not be eliminated so expeditiously from the popular as from the diplomatic mind. The fly in the ointment of Mr. Cleveland's pacifist method became now unpleasantly conspicuous; for his suggestion that British policy in South America might involve sinister designs on the Monroe Doctrine became a fixed idea with many sincere patriots. A treaty of general arbitration might, they claimed, bring sooner or later the obligation to submit the validity of this doctrine to an arbitral tribunal—a possibility that could not be contemplated save with repulsion. An additional element, moreover, in the popular prejudice against Great Britain had received much development in the revolutionary electoral campaign of 1896 in the United States. This was the year in which the movement for the free coinage of silver reached its climax and obtained the support of the Democratic Party. To the passionate propagandists of the free-silver dogma the immovable attachment of Great Britain to gold monometallism was an evidence of political depravity and reinforced the suspicion of inveterate hostility to America.

Under the influence of these and other like feelings the opposition to the arbitration treaty was strong enough, first to effect the amendment of the draft in its most essential features, and finally to deny it the approval of the American Senate. The decisive vote, on May 5, 1897, stood 43 to 26, less than two-thirds in the affirmative. Before this vote was reached the safety of the Monroe Doctrine had been insured by an amendment requiring a special agreement for the submission of any difference "which in the judgment of either power materially affects its honor or its domestic or foreign policy."

The failure of this treaty was the source of bitter disappointment to the friends of peace, official and unofficial, on both sides of the ocean. Hope had run high that the English-speaking peoples were about to pronounce decisively in favor of the principle of unrestricted arbitration and to give to this very advanced ideal the test of practical application. Even after the Senate, by amending the draft, had demolished this hope, the confidence still remained that the influence of these two powerful nations would be exerted for peace through the adoption of arbitration in some form. Failure in this also, and by a margin so narrow that a change of three votes would have made the result different, was depressing, if not wholly discouraging. It was on the scroll of fate, however, that the decisive advance toward international harmony was to come in the wake of wide-spread war. An actual agreement on arbitration followed hostilities in Cuba, in South Africa, and in the Far East.

Whether the declaration of war on Spain by the United States in the spring of 1898 was justifiable and unavoidable, will be a useful topic of debate by generations of schoolboys. There can be no room for debate, however, as to whether the war was popular in the United States. Every nerve of the nation tingled with joy that the great American democracy had at last a chance to show the spirit and power that were in it. Serious and thoughtful classes assumed with due sense of responsibility the task that had become the nation's duty. The bellicose and reckless classes greeted with ardor the opportunity for adventure and excitement. To every class, intent on the particular aspect of the situation that especially concerned it, came with thrilling satisfaction the evidence that the other English-speaking peoples were

giving their sympathy and moral support to
the Americans. The evidence was not always
of so clear and precise a character as to pass
in a court of law. Rumor and gossip and calculated lying played the part that is usual in
times of stress and excitement. There was no
room for serious doubt, however, that British
opinion was running strongly with the United
States—that an aggressive war for the acquisition of Cuba and other desirable West Indian
islands that Great Britain had always been
supposed to covet, was actually applauded by
all the leading elements of English sentiment.
Before the war was ended, numerous and highly
significant incidents confirmed the trend of
British feeling. Members of the cabinet, including even Lord Salisbury himself, publicly
praised the Americans and their mission in the
war. The leaders of the press, with a few
permanent exceptions of the ancient Tory type,
valiantly sustained the cause of the United
States against the generally violent assaults
of the Continental editors. At Manila, after
Dewey's victory suddenly raised far-reaching
problems as to the future of the Philippines, the
harassed American commander received demonstrative moral support from the British naval

force in the harbor. And when, finally, in the treaty of peace the United States, with misgivings and reluctance, took over from Spain her Far Eastern dominions, a cordial chorus of British approval greeted the assumption by the great English-speaking democracy of so considerable a share in the white man's imperialistic burden.

The effect on American opinion of these general and emphatic manifestations of sympathy and support was revolutionary. The springs of hostility to Britain that had been running full volume for a decade dried up to futile and unnoted tricklings. Mere exuberance of strength and spirit had accounted for much of this hostility, and the fighting with Spain had diverted this particular current. An uneasy sense of slighted vanity—of inadequate recognition of America's physical and moral greatness—was soothed to rest by the generous British approval of the correctness of American motives in declaring war on Spain, and by the warm welcome to the republic at its entry into the larger world-politics. If British cordiality in 1898 had been based exclusively on shrewd calculation of self-interest, it could not have been more precisely opportune. In the following year the South

African situation shaped itself into the war with the Boers. It is not hard to imagine what would have been the course of American feeling if this episode had developed three years earlier. As it was, however, reciprocity in sympathy and moral support was imperative. Those who were absorbed in the pursuit of Aguinaldo found little opportunity to carp at the harrying of Kruger. Transatlantic strictures therefore were but feeble as the two great English-speaking peoples, in Africa and the Philippines respectively, ruthlessly imposed upon backward nations the conditions of civilization and progress.

The unprecedentedly cordial relations produced by the conditions in 1898 were promptly made use of by the foreign offices in an effort to reduce the rather extensive list of unsettled differences outstanding between the two governments. Most of these involved Canada, and internal politics on both sides of the frontier happened to be just at this time propitious for adjustment. The Liberal Party won control of the Dominion government in 1896, and Sir Wilfrid Laurier, the prime minister, was anxious to try again for a system of reciprocity with the United States. At the same time President McKinley, approving though he did the excessively protectionist tariff of 1897, was definitely committed to the scheme of reciprocal arrangements for which that tariff act provided. The possibility of some agreement on this difficult but familiar subject led to the discussion of other matters, some equally familiar, others less familiar but distinctly more pressing. Among the old and well-known items were the seal fisheries of Behring Sea, the coast fisheries of the North Atlantic, and, after long quiescence, the Rush-Bagot arrangement concerning ships-of-war on the Great Lakes. Of the novel items by far the most important was the Alaskan boundary; for the discovery of gold on the Klondike River in 1896 brought a large population at once to that remote region and raised grave questions of jurisdiction where the boundary line had never been run.

For the settlement of all these and other matters a joint commission was constituted, which met at Quebec and also at Washington from August, 1898, to February, 1899. In the membership of the commission the now established policy of leaving Canadian foreign affairs chiefly to Canadians was again conspicuously illustrated; for the British representatives included five British-Americans and but one member, Lord Herschell, from across the Atlantic. The five consisted of the premiers of Canada and Newfoundland, with two other members of the Canadian cabinet, and a member of the Canadian House of Commons. The United States was represented by no less distinguished and highly qualified persons—Senators Fairbanks and Gray, Mr. Dingley, majority leader in the House of Representatives, and three experienced diplomats. All the preparations promised well for a comprehensive adjustment, and roseate reports of progress attended the work of the commission. On February 20, however, a recess was taken, which gradually became recognized as permanent. The sessions were never resumed, and the chief cause of this unfortunate outcome was the inability of the two governments to agree about the Alaskan boundary.

This last of the boundary disputes that filled the hundred years of peace with contention had all the familiar characteristics of its predecessors. The line dividing Russian from British America was described in the treaties that fixed it as following the summit of the mountains situated parallel to the coast between two designated points of latitude and longitude;

where the mountains should prove to be more than ten leagues from the ocean, the line should run parallel to the coast at a distance of ten leagues from it. Mountains such as the treaties called for, the Americans could not find; Canadian geographers found them in adequate abundance and very near to the ocean. As to the "coast" from which the ten leagues were to be measured, the difference of opinion was no less marked. To the Americans the term meant continental land, with all the sinuosities and indentations with which the region abounded, so that the boundary should never come within thirty miles of tide-water; to the Canadians the coast-line was a wholly different thing, to be run by the general trend of the land, and to be determined on occasion by the headlands of inlets, or by offshore islands, so that the boundary would often cross considerable stretches of tide-water.

There was no concealment of the practical issue that lay behind the technical contentions of the two parties. The American position excluded Canada absolutely from contact with the ocean anywhere on the Pacific coast north of the southernmost point of Alaska; the Canadian claim insured to Canada a seaport on the arm of the ocean that afforded the most practicable access to the Klondike gold-fields, which were mostly on Canadian soil. The interests at stake were very great and the conflict was correspondingly stubborn. When agreement became impossible in the conferences of the commission, the British representatives offered arbitration, but the Americans refused consent to any form of tribunal that left the decision to an umpire, and the British rejected as futile any tribunal that might be deadlocked. In such an *impasse* there was no recourse but to give up the matter, since the Canadians had consented to the commission largely in the expectation of a favorable outcome on this point, and had been ready to make substantial concessions in other directions in order to attain their purpose here.

The inauspicious result of this first attempt to reap a crop of adjustments from the international cordiality produced by the Spanish War did not prevent a further cultivation of the field. Apparently the first attempt had been too ambitious—had sought returns of too diverse a character. Taken one at a time instead of collectively, the problems calling for solution might be more successfully handled.

Such seems to have been the conclusion reached
by the British and American Governments, and
the procedure in accordance with which it was
put in practice effected smoothly and harmoni-
ously the remarkable series of agreements that
brought the century of peace to a close in unprecedented good feeling.  The era had come
of a singularly sane and gifted series of personalities in control of American foreign affairs.
John Hay, after distinguished success at the
court of Saint James's, became in 1899 head of
the Department of State at Washington.  Joseph H. Choate succeeded Hay as ambassador
at London.  Elihu Root, after indispensable
service in other positions, took over the Department of State at the death of Hay in 1905.
To these men on the American side, with
Salisbury, Lansdowne, and Grey at the British
Foreign Office, and Pauncefote and James
Bryce in the British embassy at Washington,
is to be ascribed in a particular degree, though
without disparagement of others, the confirmation of that deep amity with which the
century of peace came to a close.

The decade following 1898 shows a far larger
total of diplomatic agreements between Great
Britain and the United States than any other

decade in history.  First, the disturbing boundary of Alaska was removed from the foreground till the disagreeable feelings aroused by
it should have time to subside.  A *modus
vivendi* was put into effect in October, 1899,
fixing a provisional line at the points where
friction was most imminent and protecting all
rights and claims of both parties pending the
definitive settlement.

Soon followed the announcement of negotiations peculiarly calculated to give satisfaction
to the Americans.  The Clayton-Bulwer Treaty
of 1850, hailed as a momentous triumph of
American diplomacy when it was concluded, had
become later offensive to the national pride.
It obligated the United States to refrain from
exclusive control of the proposed Nicaragua
Canal, and to insure the safety and neutrality
of that or any other transisthmian communication only in association with Great Britain.
During the half-century that had elapsed since
the conclusion of this treaty, the interests and
the power of the United States had taken such
form that no canal was likely to be actually
constructed except in accordance with her will.
The restrictions on this will embodied in the
Clayton-Bulwer agreement were not only a

source of exasperation to American feelings, but were also a grave obstacle to the construction of a canal. A strong sentiment prevailed that no canal at all was preferable to one over which Great Britain should have joint control. Especially in view of the recent extension given to the Monroe Doctrine, the intrusion of a European power in the affairs of the isthmus was resented as intolerable.

Under the circumstances, the willingness of Great Britain to abandon her rights under the Clayton-Bulwer Treaty was a very great step in the promotion of good feeling. Yet the mode of abandonment was subjected to diligent, not to say suspicious, scrutiny by the American Senate. Secretary Hay and Sir Julian Pauncefote concluded a treaty in February, 1900, that the Senate refused to approve except with amendments. In this draft Great Britain renounced all right to participate in the construction, ownership, or maintenance of a canal, but assumed jointly with the United States, and such other powers as should be willing, responsibility for the neutrality of the work. Eventually the American extremists had their way, and the United States was left in sole control of neutralization as well as of construction and maintenance. A new convention was concluded by Messrs. Hay and Pauncefote November 18, 1901, and duly ratified, under which the Clayton-Bulwer Treaty was formally "superseded," and the United States was left with an entirely free hand in respect to any transisthmian canal, save that the general principle of neutralization was declared to be left unimpaired, and the American Government formally adopted as the basis of neutralization the rules which were in force as to the Suez Canal.

A little over a year after this notable achievement Secretary Hay and Sir Michael Herbert, Pauncefote's successor at the embassy, signed a convention sending the Alaskan boundary to arbitration. The tribunal agreed upon was of the sort that the United States had been willing to accept in 1899, namely, a joint commission of six jurists, three designated by each government. Such a tribunal was duly constituted, Great Britain being represented by the Lord Chief-Justice Baron Alverstone and two distinguished Canadians, the United States by the Secretary of War Mr. Root and two prominent Senators. A decision was announced by this tribunal October 20, 1903, in which all the seriously contested points were determined in favor of the United States, by a majority consisting of Lord Alverstone and the three Americans.

Thus passed finally to rest the boundary contention that had tried the tempers of the English-speaking peoples continuously since the beginning of their history as neighbors. Until some new and unforeseen acquisition of territory by one or the other of the nations shall take place, no further differences of this sort seem possible. Every yard of the four-thousand-mile line along which the British and American domains are contiguous, from the Bay of Fundy to the point where the 141st meridian intersects the shore of the Arctic Ocean, is now fixed, and most of them marked, by the most precise methods known to modern science. Yet eternal vigilance alone can assure the maintenance of the certainty that has been provided. It was, in fact, one incident of the era of good international feeling that we are describing that Messrs. Bryce and Root were able to conclude in 1908 a convention providing for the verification and re-marking of the line from the eastern extremity to the Pacific.

This *annus mirabilis* of diplomatic achievement produced also a convention that secured

to American and Canadian officers of the law
having prisoners in their custody reciprocal
rights of transit across one another's territory,
and further removed the rather mediæval restrictions imposed by the customs laws of the
two governments upon the rendering of aid to
disabled mariners, in waters traversed by the
international boundary, by vessels belonging
on the other side of the line. It became a
new bond uniting the English-speaking peoples,
that through the efforts of Messrs. Root and
Bryce a Canadian captain on Lake Erie might
go to the aid of a disabled ship in American
water without exposure to heavy penalties under
the laws of the United States.

Four other conventions marked this period.
The only one that need detain us was that
through which a definite term was put to the
controversies touching the North Atlantic fisheries. After the sharp clash in the eighties[1]
between the United States and Canada, there
followed nearly twenty years of substantial
calm. Not till 1905 was there a revival of
trouble. In that year the government of Newfoundland gave up the practice of licensing the
American fishermen and assumed toward them

[1] See above, p. 278.

an attitude that raised anew all the old controversies. The colony sought to prescribe
regulations for fishing, even on the treaty coast,
that were held by the Americans to be wholly
destructive to their business. Diplomacy in-
tervened and, by resort to a new *modus vivendi*,
preserved the peace until an agreement to arbi-
trate was arrived at. The procedure of the
British Government in this matter aroused
sharp resentment in Newfoundland, and conformity by the colonial authorities to the
prescriptions of the cabinet at London was
insured only by a threat of force.

While this situation was giving cause for
vexation, Messrs. Root and Bryce, in the course
of their treaty-making progress, signed on April
8, 1908, an arbitration convention that succeeded in winning the approval of the American
Senate. It was no such broad and comprehensive agreement as that framed by Olney and
Pauncefote in 1897. Yet it served its purpose in the trend of world movement; for it
took its form under the influence and pre-
scription of The Hague Conference, and expressed the concurrence of the English-speaking
peoples in the beneficent work of that assembly.
By the treaty a dispute concerning the inter-

pretation of a treaty is to be referred by a special agreement to the permanent Court of Arbitration at The Hague. Such agreement must in the United States be submitted to the Senate for approval, and in Great Britain may be subject to the concurrence of any self-governing dominion whose interests are affected by the matter at issue. That the fisheries dispute fell within the provisions of this arbitration treaty, and that the fact was keenly present to the minds of the negotiators, may be inferred from the fact that under the same date as the signature of the treaty a special agreement under its provisions was signed by Messrs. Root and Bryce, referring to The Hague Tribunal the interpretation of the fisheries article of the treaty of 1818 between the United States and Great Britain. This agreement, put in effect by exchange of notes March 4, 1909, insured a settlement of practically all the issues of this century-old controversy.

The presentation of the case to the tribunal took place in the summer of 1910, and the decision was made on September 7 of that year. By the terms of the arbitration the judgment of the tribunal was called for on seven questions. In these were summed up the chief points in the long controversies between the two governments. The character of the tribunal's answers is a conclusive refutation of the charges, made throughout the century of conflict by hotheads on each side, that its rights were so clear as to leave deliberate aggression the only explanation of the acts of the other side. On practically every point the judgment of the tribunal was so framed as to recognize merit in the contention of each side.

The decision on all the issues was accepted with perfect good temper by all parties. It was decided that Canada and Newfoundland had the right to make reasonable regulations for the fishing on the shores to which the Americans had access by treaty; but in case of dispute as to what was reasonable, neither of the governments concerned, but an impartial tribunal, must have the authority to answer the question. It was decided that Americans fishing on the treaty shores might hire natives to aid in the work, but that the natives so employed did not thereby gain immunity from the laws of the jurisdiction, or, in terms of the concrete situation involved: the American fishermen had the right to man their ships with Newfound-

landers, as was the general practice, and the
colonial government had the right to prohibit
the Newfoundlanders to serve and punish them
for serving, as was also becoming a practice.
It was decided that the American fishermen
ought not to be subjected to the custom-house
requirements and harbor dues that applied to
commercial shipping; that they were not,
however, excluded from the privileges of commercial shipping, provided that they did not
try to enjoy the liberty of fishing and the privilege of trading at the same time. Finally,
on the very important question as to what
constituted "bays," in the sense in which the
Americans had by treaty the right to fish in
them, it was decided that where the arm of the
sea did not exceed ten miles in width at its
mouth, the coast-line should be considered as
running from headland to headland, while
elsewhere it should follow the sinuosities of the
shore, save that for a considerable number of
indentations the shore line at their mouths was
specifically described in the decision.

The result of this arbitration, completed by
the supplementary proceedings called for, left
apparently no opportunity for a renewal of
friction in connection with the Atlantic fish-

eries. As to the seals in the Pacific Ocean, whose diminishing numbers at the breeding-places in the Behring Sea gave great concern to the United States, an agreement was reached in the summer of 1911 by the four powers chiefly concerned, Great Britain, the United States, Russia, and Japan, prohibiting pelagic hunting for a period of fifteen years. This involved the temporary extinction of a large industry of British Columbia in order to avoid the utter destruction of the fur-seals.

By this time no controverted question of right remained to make trouble so far as concerned the relations of the United States and Canada. Commercial policy offered, however, as for the last half-century, inviting opportunities for modifications and improvements. In both countries there were indications of serious discontent with the existing high tariffs. The American revision of 1909 was followed by an overwhelming defeat of the Republicans in the elections, in which tariff questions played a large part. Sir Wilfrid Laurier, prime minister of the Dominion, thereupon entered vigorously upon negotiations with the American Government for a reciprocal reduction of duties on the commodities most involved in the commerce between Canada and the United States. An agreement was reached with astonishing ease, considering the peremptory rejection of earlier proposals, and a very far-reaching reduction of rates was scheduled, subject to the approval of the respective legislatures. At Washington this approval was readily secured; at Ottawa it was opposed with vehemence, and on appeal to the constituencies the government met with an overwhelming defeat. Canada thus rejected with something of contempt an arrangement that would have brought her enormous economic benefits—an arrangement that she had often sought with almost humble diligence from the United States.

The decisive factor in bringing about this abrupt reversal of Canadian policy was the spirit of nationality. Inept comments by prominent American statesmen on the situation during the electoral campaign were diligently interpreted in Canada to mean that the ready assent to reciprocity was a first deliberate step towards annexation. Again, as in 1891, the Canadian people declared for political independence in preference to economic ease, as they conceived that alternative to be placed before them. Nor did it lie in the mouths of the Americans to chide or reproach; for every argument, whether sound or merely silly, that was used in Canada to resist the demand for freer trade with the United States had been used with effect in the United States, in a dozen campaigns, to resist the demand for freer trade with Great Britain. The national spirit was producing in Canada the identical phenomena that had attended the growth of the United States to its magnificent estate of independence and power. Hence no bad blood was made by the failure of reciprocity. The Americans looked serenely on while the great Dominion displayed the same spirit, in maintaining economic independence at the end of the century of peace, that the little Canadian provinces had displayed at the beginning of that century, in maintaining their political and military independence.

The harmony between Britain and America was the leading factor in another effort to promote the cause of general arbitration. With the seriously qualified success of this undertaking the diplomatic record of the hundred years of peace was substantially completed. In the summer of 1911 a form of agreement was devised which referred to arbitral procedure all international controversies that were "justici-

able." Treaties embodying this agreement were
concluded by the United States with Great
Britain and also with France. But the objections that found their home in the American
Senate were too strong to be overcome. That
body gave its approval of the treaties only after
amending them so as to make each party for itself the final judge as to whether a dispute was
justiciable, and further excluding altogether
from the provisions of the treaties several cat-
egories of differences, notably those involving
the Monroe Doctrine. These amendments left
the treaties barren of all the advance that had
been hoped for toward general arbitration.

Such was the situation when the centennial
of the Treaty of Ghent drew near. The sharp
exchange of notes about the Venezuelan boundary in 1895 had been followed by the establishment of ostentatiously cordial diplomatic relations between the two great English-speaking
nations; and this had been followed in turn,
after the outbreak of the Spanish War, by
demonstrations of good feeling, both official
and unofficial, that were quite unprecedented
for warmth as well as for generality. The few
discordant notes—in America over the fate of
the Boers, in Canada over the outcome of the

Alaskan boundary arbitration, among Irishmen
perennially and everywhere—were barely discoverable by the acutest observers amid the
multifold chorus of amity.

There was especial significance in this situation from the fact that it was accompanied
by a remarkable transformation in the ideals
and principles of both British and American
political systems. In the last quarter of the
century of peace his Britannic Majesty's dominions became very distinctly a federative
empire, and the United States became no less
unmistakably an imperialistic republic. The
earliest evidence of a tendency in these directions had been the occasion of reciprocal resentment and hostility on the part of Great Britain
and the United States. The southern and
westward expansion of the American Republic
in the first half of the nineteenth century caused,
as we have seen, much uneasiness and dissat-
isfaction to the British Government; yet the
absorption of the Spanish dominions in the
West Indies and the Far East at the century's
end evoked that government's cordial approval.
So on the other side the earlier steps toward
the development and utilization of Canadian
resources for distinctively imperial purposes

was followed with truculence in the United States; while the later creation of the strongest commercial and political bonds between the United Kingdom and the Dominion has been viewed with placid content. It would seem to augur well for the perpetuity of peace between the greatest of the English-speaking peoples, that each approves the policy that enhances the power and prestige of the other. The general causes that have operated to produce this situation are worthy of brief consideration; for in them we shall see again the forces that have from the beginning of our century wrought for English-speaking harmony, despite all the temporary influences that have from time to time prevailed against them.

The distinct assumption by the United States of the imperialistic character and responsibilities coincided precisely in time with the warmest manifestations of cordiality on the part of Great Britain. President Roosevelt's administrations (1901–09) teemed with incidents announcing the new rôle of the American Republic. The Philippines were relentlessly reduced to order and subjection; Panama was "taken" for the sake of the world's commerce, if incidentally for the specific military and commercial advantage of the taker; Cuba was summarily denied by superior force indulgence in her long-wonted pastime of civil war—all these by virtue of conditions produced directly by the war with Spain.  Indirect results of this war were no less striking.  American troops joined with those of other great powers in quelling the tumult of the "Boxers" in China, and American diplomacy wrought effectively to maintain the open door in Chinese trade and the very existence ("administrative entity," Secretary Hay obscurely called it) of native government in China, when the rivalry of Russia and Japan threatened it with extinction.  The terrific clash of arms between these two powers was brought to an end on the soil of the United States and through the agency of its chief executive.  It became suddenly apparent to all the world that the American democracy was a force of the first magnitude in the general international situation.

The effect of this revelation was not without its humor to the philosophical observer.  In the world and the half-world of universal politics rumor and gossip ran wild over the possible results of the new phenomenon.  Veteran diplomats saw copious visions and retired admirals dreamed horrid dreams. Periodical literature teemed with speculation as to the influence of the American position on the various *ententes* and numerical alliances, dual, triple, quadruple, on which the peace of the world was supposed to rest. The navy of the United States was taken in hand by the theoretical experts, and subjected to the mathematical scrutiny from which the guild derives its sufficient conclusions as to future relations of the nations. Almost before the Treaty of Portsmouth was ratified, the prophets had the broad breast of the Pacific tumultuous with the rivalry of America and Japan and convulsed with hypothetical battles. The results on the combatants and the wider effects on mankind at large naturally varied with the fancy of the prophets, but in no case were unworthy of the occasion, or failed to involve a startling change in the political equilibrium of the world.

Amid all the disquiet and suspicion created by the entrance of the United States upon its new rôle, there was no deviation on the part of Great Britain from the attitude of admiring welcome to the republic. No prognostications of disastrous rivalry wherein the pride of Britain would be humbled—and there was abundance of such warnings—availed to stir up jealousy or fear. The grounds of British complacency were, of course, manifold. That the Americans, in assuming dominion over less developed races, would be forced to solve some problems by the same methods that had brought harsh criticism upon the British, was so certain as to be a source of some natural satisfaction. The course of events in the Philippines very quickly confirmed this feeling. Beyond all such reasons, however, the source of British approval of American policy was a genuine joy that through it English institutions and traditions, however modified by transmission through the United States, were to be extended still further in their remarkable progress over the world.

Meanwhile this progress was reacting in a noteworthy manner on the complex political aggregate known as the British Empire. Till the ninth decade of the nineteenth century it remained the basic conviction of reflecting politicians in England that the destiny of the self-governing colonies was independence. The grip of Cobden's dogma was strong twenty years after he himself had passed away. No way of escape from disintegration of the empire

could be thought of that did not involve unthinkable readjustments in the government of
the United Kingdom, as to structure or policy
or both.  In the eighties, however, conditions
in both foreign and domestic affairs brought
the unthinkable peremptorily under consideration.  Germany's colonial ambitions and
Russia's advance on India suggested sickening
possibilities as to the fate of an Australasian
state that should lack the protection of the
British navy; Gladstone's proposal of home
rule for Ireland made the remodelling of the
British Government a staple of daily debate.
Under these circumstances a demand for some
strengthening of the bonds uniting colonies
and motherland became vigorously manifest
throughout her Majesty's dominions.

The formula of this demand in the eighties
was "imperial federation," on behalf of which
an imposing agitation was carried on for some
years.  Official support for this particular form
of union was for various practical reasons slow
and scanty, and the movement under this
name lost its force in the early nineties, not
without having contributed, however, a great
impulse to the cause of preserving the empire
intact.  Meanwhile a procedure for the discus-

sion and solution of pressing concrete problems opened a way through which, *more Britannico*, the broad considerations of constitutional theory were sidetracked and imperial consolidation was approached by the slow but sure pathway of extra-constitutional experiment. In 1887, on the occasion of Queen Victoria's jubilee, a conference of colonial representatives was held at London under the auspices of the colonial secretary. Its consultations were of little effect save in revealing a basis of common interest in the widely scattered members of the empire. As was prophesied by Lord Salisbury, however, this meeting became "the parent of a long progeniture"; for such conferences have become an established feature of the imperial system, assembling every four years, and acting under a well-defined constitution. This imperial conference is, in fact, a new and significant organ of policy and administration for his British Majesty's dominions. In its deliberations have taken shape the policies which in recent years have done so much to increase the force of the British Empire. The obstacles to be overcome, in the shape of conflicting interests and the spirit of local independence, have not availed to thwart the trend toward imperial unity. A general system of naval and military organization and action has been put into operation; tariff preferences, varying in scope and volume, have been generally established in reciprocity among the subordinate members of the empire, with the United Kingdom enjoying in most cases a unilateral advantage; a great impulse has been given to exclusively British lines of communication and transportation. These and many other instances of consolidating activity reveal the widely scattered dominions of the British crown, though geographically so discontinuous, as a very effective unity.

In the process through which imperial unity has been practically realized there has been a mighty, if subtle, reaction of the colonial spirit upon the motherland. Canada, South Africa, Australia, New Zealand are democratic in their social structure and their political ideals. Two of them embody the most advanced democracies in the world. An imperial council in which a leading part is played by the chosen representatives of such communities must inevitably take color in its resolutions from the programme of radicalism. The colonial secretary who goes from a discussion in the imperial conference to a debate on social legislation in the House of Commons can hardly fail to carry with him some infection of the ideas that are current coin in Australia. Wherever the delegates from beyond the seas are brought in contact unofficially with the political issues most agitated in the United Kingdom, it is not the conservative views that are supported by the recitals of experience in the colonies. What to the English radical is ultimate ideal, to the colonial conservative is a commonplace of actuality. Even Irish home rule, that smacks so perilously of disintegration to many of the wisest minds of England, offers nothing of terror to the colonial; for he sees autonomy and unity reconciled in diverse but sufficient ways, in the Dominion of Canada, the Commonwealth of Australia, and the Union of South Africa. Popular self-government is so fundamental in the political philosophy of the English beyond the seas that the full application of the principle to the United Kingdom appears only normal. A Canadian or an Australian is not likely to see anything alarming in a project for the transformation of the government of the United Kingdom in the federal sense; while the union of all parts of the British world under something in the nature of a federative bond makes a strong appeal to every English-speaking group that treasures the traditions and achievements of the race.

By every step toward the closer union of the scattered parts of the British Empire the more general solidarity of the English-speaking peoples has been brought nearer. For every such step signalizes the democratizing *pro tanto* of social and political ideals and institutions in the United Kingdom, and the realization thus of conditions that promote harmony with the American Republic. An intimate like-mindedness is, as was said at the beginning of this review, the indispensable factor in permanent international amity. The whole trend of modern development in civilization is strongly toward the widespread working of this factor. Its influence is most marked, however, where historical identity of language and tradition clears the way. The people of the United Kingdom and the people of the United States are drawing nearer each other daily in both the material and the spiritual aspects of life. What has been expected to retard, has in fact accelerated the movement. Nervous Britons strike out for a closer union of all the parts of the empire, to check the influence of the United States—and the result is an access of democracy from Australia that makes American ideas inviting by comparison. Americans rush into war to uphold the cause of humanity and independence for oppressed peoples—and find themselves struggling to carry, in the most approved British manner, the burden of distant and barbarous dependencies. But the federative empire of the Britons and the imperialistic republic of the Americans are more neighborly after than before their transforming experiments.

The hundred years of peace for which John Quincy Adams politely, if not very hopefully, prayed after the signing of the treaty of December 24, 1814, have become realized history. The gates of Janus, closed at Ghent, have not been opened for a century. The pacific years have brought changes, however, more amazing than could have been wrought by the desolating arts of war. It is not so clear in the twentieth as it was in the nineteenth century that the nerve centre of the English-speaking world is in Great Britain. The United Kingdom, with its 45,000,000 of population, is a wonderful aggregate of ma-

terial and spiritual forces. Yet it does not
stand out so incontestably the chief reservoir
of such forces as was the case a century earlier,
when it numbered but 19,000,000 souls. Then
it dominated the English-speaking peoples of
the earth commercially, industrially, intellec-
tually, and, save the United States, politically. Its dependencies were already vast in
extent, but none contained more inhabitants
of British origin than Canada, where there
were hardly 250,000. To-day the dependencies include, in addition to Canada, with its
7,500,000 people, Australia, with some 4,500,-
000, New Zealand, with 1,000,000, and South
Africa, with another 1,000,000 of whites, among
whom the English type is somewhat modified
by the Dutch. The reaction of these great
progressive communities upon the mother-land
is altogether too significant to be disregarded,
and it is growing from year to year. Domination, in any such sense as was accurate in
1814, cannot be predicated of the United
Kingdom. It is now but the most powerful
member of a larger unity, the British Empire,
already in fact, and rapidly becoming in name,
a federation of English-speaking states.

Outside of this political and cultural aggregate the English-speaking world presents only the American Republic. Its population, nearly 100,000,000, includes probably three-fifths of the English-speaking people of the earth, fifty per cent more than inhabit the British Empire. Geographically the United States presents the most striking contrast with that empire—the one territorially continuous, the other a series of widely scattered areas. Socially, economically, and politically the contrasts, while apparently great, shrink remarkably on close examination. Institutions that characterize the old, wealthy, and highly developed society of England have appeared, at least in rudimentary form, in many of the first-settled, richer, and more prosperous States of the American Union. The institutions, on the other hand, that are typical of the sparse and primitive communities of Canada, Australia, and South Africa have their perfect counterpart on the plains and arid plateaus in the western half of the United States. Between the American people and the people of the British Empire as a whole there are the political and cultural conditions of a complete understanding and sympathy. History and traditions, when properly interpreted, must contribute to the same end.   There seems no reason, therefore, to suppose that the next hundred years will show less progress than the last in cordial relations among the English-speaking peoples.

# CHAPTER VIII

## CONCLUSION

The discussion of international relations is almost invariably tainted with the fallacy of too sweeping generalization. This is as true of historical as of argumentative discussion. It has been copiously illustrated in the events narrated in the preceding chapters. It may doubtless be found illustrated by the narrative itself; for the vice inheres in the very structure and function of language. A crisis or a policy of vital import to the English-speaking peoples has more than once had its origin in some jaunty judgment that Great Britain despised the United States, or that Canada was enamoured of annexation, or that America hated the English, when in truth the emotions referred to could be predicated only of some individual or group in the respective nations. The editor of the London *Times* or *The Saturday Review* has been taken for Great Britain, Goldwin Smith for Canada, and any one of a dozen

357

politicians of Celtic extraction or sympathies for America. These and similar identifications have figured largely in the historical writings of the century, with distracting results. There has been on the whole overemphasis on the evidences of ill feeling among the English-speaking peoples. The influence of the episodes that gave rise to diplomatic friction has been exaggerated. Forces that worked unceasingly and powerfully for good feeling have been ignored. An ingrained diplomatic policy, a strong and popular personality, an expedient of party strategy or a demand of an insistent economic interest has been treated as a conclusive index of the national spirit, whereas such spirit is justly discoverable only in a careful synthesis of these elements. Surveyed with proper reference to this fact, our review of the century of peace may be summarized as follows:

The hundred years fall into four fairly well distinguishable periods. In the first, 1814–1835, the key to Anglo-American relations is to be found in Great Britain's foreign policy in Europe and her internal politics. In the second, 1836–1860, the controlling feature is the growth of the United States in population and territory. The third, 1861–1885, takes its character from the American Civil War. The fourth, 1886–1914, turns on the projection of American and British interests and influence beyond the bounds of the United States and the United Kingdom.

In the first period there was a gradual progress from the bitterness that the war made intense in America and Canada to a condition of general amity. The Treaty of Ghent put an end to flagrant war; it did little or nothing for the promotion of lasting peace. It did not weaken the conviction in the minds of many Americans that a leading principle of British policy was to bully and dragoon the United States into a condition of dependence as near as possible to that which had been thrown off in 1776; it did not extinguish the fear among the English in Canada that the United States was resolutely bent on conquering and annexing them; it did not qualify the belief widespread among the ruling aristocracy in England that the American democracy was a barbarous, brawling political organism, whose growth was to be restricted by all possible means in the interest of civilization. For each of these various beliefs there was not lacking a certain foundation in fact; and the progress toward amity was measured by the transformation of the facts.

The diplomacy of this period made some important contributions to the perpetuation of the peace secured at Ghent. The Rush-Bagot arrangement was the chief of them. An influential element of American opinion was conciliated by the limited access to the inshore fisheries conceded by Great Britain in 1818, though the concession embodied potentialities of trouble. So far as the Monroe Doctrine may be regarded as a product of diplomacy, it must stand high in the records of this period. Whether its function was pacific, or ever will be so, is doubtful. At the time of its announcement, however, it unquestionably promoted good feeling between the British and the American peoples. A like effect was produced by the modification in commercial policy through which the bars were let down for the American traders in the West Indies. On the other side was felt throughout the period the exasperating operation of the failure to get together on the right of search and in respect to the northeastern boundary of the United States. No amount of concession by the British Government on other points could keep down the

American's gorge at the thought that the right was still claimed to inflict on American vessels and seamen the humiliations that were common before 1815. This feeling in the United States and the irritation in Canada and New Brunswick over what was felt to be the unfounded claims of the Americans as to the boundary were the chief factors of popular ill feeling that survived to the end of this first period. The spectacular triumphs of the Whigs over the Tories in the United Kingdom tended greatly to reduce the springs of animosity among the Americans in reference to the British in general.

Our second period began with trouble, and trouble among the English-speaking peoples was continuous almost to the end. There was insurrection in Canada and exasperating border incidents. The northeastern boundary produced a grist of friction and popular excitement. Antislavery authorities in the British West Indies took doubtful liberties with American slaves and ships. The singular sequence of serious controversies dissipated the general friendliness and introduced a persistent condition of distrust and acrimony. Webster and Ashburton succeeded in settling the northeastern boundary and some other points of contention, but many were left, including the right of search. The American democracy was fully embarked on its career of expansion. Led by the men of the mighty West, it proceeded to realize its "manifest destiny" in Texas, in Oregon, and in California. Half the total coast of the Gulf of Mexico and half the total Pacific coast of North America were the modest limits of its demands. Great Britain, congenital mistress of the seas and sovereign over Canada and the Hudson's Bay Company, had necessarily to take notice of these proceedings. She saved part of Oregon, but her projects for Texas and California gave way before the resolute aggression of Polk. Through the war with Mexico the United States realized its alleged destiny. In the very month in which peace was concluded the golden secret of the Sierras was disclosed at Sutter's Mill, and the adventurous of all the earth started for California. At once the Central American isthmus became one of the greatest highways of the world, and as promptly appeared the clash between British and American claims and interests in Nicaragua. The Clayton-Bulwer Treaty, and ten years of harassing negotiation to determine what it meant, followed this development.

The events on which these two decades of diplomacy turned were replete with incidents that stirred the passions of the peoples and made much bad blood between them. At the same time other events in the national life of all concerned worked clearly for friendship and good feeling. Free trade became the commercial policy of both Great Britain and the United States. The whole democratic spirit of Cobden and Bright became influential in British politics and won the approval of Americans. Palmerston's foreign policy after 1848, whatever its inconsistencies, was at least favorable to the Liberals of the Continent. In this again American opinion was conciliated. The exiled heroes of unsuccessful revolt on the Continent—Kossuth, Garibaldi, Schurz—found equal welcome in England and the United States; and those who gave the welcome could not but feel drawn to each other. Common sympathy with Magyars and Italians and Germans tended somewhat to counteract the effect of the wide divergence of sympathies in respect to the Irish. Canadians and Americans, whose antipathies rose high at the beginning of this period, were at its close once more on cordial terms through the Reciprocity Treaty of 1854. There was indeed, in 1860, a general spirit of trans-Atlantic friendliness among the English-speaking peoples, to which the visit of the youthful Prince of Wales in the United States and Canada was a witness. The American Republic itself was, however, permeated with the animosities of the sections, and the fiercest antipathies that ever divided English-speaking peoples were about to be manifested in the conflict between North and South.

The period of the American Civil War was one of utter distraction, as to both feeling and convictions, among the English-speaking peoples. From the outset there was in both the warring sections as much fear and distrust of Great Britain as hatred of each other. British sentiment was at the same time almost as badly divided as American. No assertion could be more inaccurate than that the British in general favored the South. There was a large and influential body of Southern sympathizers, moved by the conviction that the secession rested on a just claim to independence and self-government. There was an equally convinced body of Northern sympathizers, moved by hatred of slavery and hope that it would be extinguished. In both these bodies alike the prevailing expectation was, till late in the course of the struggle, that the disruption of the American Republic would be permanent. This expectation, rather than sympathy with the South, was the basis of Gladstone's declaration, proclaimed with such shocking indiscretion at Newcastle, that Jefferson Davis had created a nation, and of Edward A. Freeman's famous title-page, "History of Federal Government . . . to the Disruption of the United States." Satisfied that but one outcome was possible, the great mass of British sentiment watched with but the sightseer's interest the course of events through which the inevitable end was to be reached. This attitude was the substantial foundation of the government's policy of neutrality. The good faith of Palmerston and Russell in the assumption of this policy is now beyond question; the lack of entire success in its execution is equally clear. The South complained as bitterly as the North of British policy; only the victorious North got satisfaction. If the South had established its independence, Great Britain might have had double grievances to settle for. As it was, she settled with more grace than could fairly be anticipated the cost of her errors in respect to the North. Whatever grounds she had for contesting the claims of the United States, her position was almost hopelessly weakened from the outset by the staring fact that the result of the American war was precisely that which highly respected leaders of British opinion had assumed to be impossible.

The Treaty of Washington of 1871, with the arbitrations that followed, signified the recognition by the other English-speaking peoples that the American Republic was a new and permanent species of political organism. It signified the acceptance of democracy as a respectable mode of national existence. It marked the transition in British politics from the régime of Whigs and Tories to that of Liberals and Conservatives, from Palmerston and Russell to Gladstone and Bright, from Aberdeen and Derby to Disraeli and Salisbury. Throughout the English-speaking world the democratic spirit was visibly transforming institutions. In the United Kingdom it gave the suffrage to a million hitherto excluded men of the working class, made education more accessible to the poor, began the transfer of the land of Ireland from the aristocracy to the Irish tenant farmers. In the United States it raised four millions of negroes from chattel slavery to civil and political equality with their former masters. In Australia and British America it dominated in every respect the great expansion of these communities that characterized the period. The Dominion of Canada was established, to parallel on the north of the United States the development of free institutions across the continent. With whatever disparity of population and resources, the new Dominion exhibited as distinctly as its great neighbor the qualities of a progressive, independent, and self-sufficient democracy.

Our fourth period opens with friction between the two neighbors in North America. Both peoples were in the course of marvellous internal development. The two oceans were bound together by railways and the vast interior spaces of the continent were becoming peopled and prosperous on both sides of the astronomical line that alone marked them off as distinct. Along all the thousands of miles of this line no incident occurred to arouse the concern of the governments, but the tide-water

at each end of it was in the eighties stirred with
conflict. On the Atlantic the inshore fisheries
again caused trouble; on the Pacific the fur-
seals of Alaska. Both disputes were duly settled by rational administration and finally by
arbitration. Then came the successive manifestations of American self-consciousness in
connection with Samoa, Hawaii, Chile, Cuba.
A restless, sensitive condition of the popular
mind was discernible to an acute observer.
The British Foreign Office for some reason failed
to note this phenomenon. Likewise unno-
ticed was the coincidence of a high-strung and
irritable chief executive at Washington with a
cynical *quondam Saturday Review* essayist as
foreign minister in Downing Street. The internal politics of both nations contributed conditions that favored an explosion, and the
explosion duly occurred.

Cleveland's policy as to the Venezuelan
boundary announced to the world, with seismic
suddenness and violence, that the American
democracy was of age. Its cherished Monroe
Doctrine was declared the basis of much the
same authority that European powers were
assuming in Africa and Asia through the doctrines of *Hinterland* and "sphere of influence."

Once recovered from the shock caused by the occasion and manner of the announcement, the British Government and the British people were the first to recognize the new situation and to welcome it. The maintenance of peace and amity between the English-speaking nations became the goal of official and unofficial effort on both sides of the ocean. With the Spanish-American War came the convincing demonstrations of good feeling on the part of the British for the United States. From this event dates unbroken cordiality to the end of the hundred years of peace. Diplomacy, directly or through arbitration, settled all the old disputes that threatened tension. Progress was made toward the comprehensive substitution of pacific for warlike means in dealing with all kinds of controversies. Canada waxed great and prosperous on the frontier of the United States, and proclaimed an unmistakable purpose to remain the rival rather than become in any sense the appendage of the republic; Australia, New Zealand, South Africa developed into progressive democratic commonwealths; and all these powerful political societies moved steadily toward closer union with the United Kingdom in an earth-girdling federative empire. Each step in the consolidation of this mighty structure has received in the United States the same degree of cordial approval that Great Britain displayed when the United States set forth on its imperialistic career among the ruins of the Spanish dominion.

The century of peace ends with the English-speaking world comprehended in two great political aggregates, differing much from each other in obvious characteristics, but permeated in the subtler arteries of their social life with forces that make for like feeling and like thinking. The same basic conceptions of democracy, liberty, and law prevail in both these organisms and determine the direction of conscious progress; the growing parallelism of economic conditions, the long-established financial and commercial relationships, the intimate solidarity of intellectual life, assure that the lines of unconscious progress will be the same in both. Everything seems to promise the absence of all but friendly rivalry in reciprocal benefits and in contribution to the welfare of the race.

Our historical review has shown that in the relation of the English-speaking peoples there has been much misconception, distrust, suspi-

cion, and general incompatibility of temper—
that these peoples have been in a high degree
human. But it has also shown that they have
exhibited, on a steadily growing scale, that
loftiest of human attributes—the will to adjust
the frictions of social life by reason, the faculty
that President Butler has so well designated, in
its broadest aspect, as "the international mind."
Our review has shown finally, if it has been adequate and truthful, that there has persisted in
the consciousness of these peoples, often enough
obscurely, but none the less certainly, the feeling that some special fiat of God and nature en-
joins enduring peace among those whose blood
or language or institutions or traditions, or
all together, go back historically to the snug
little island of Britain.

# INDEX

DATE DUE